Misreadings

Misreadings

Umberto Eco

**TRANSLATED FROM THE ITALIAN
BY WILLIAM WEAVER**

First published in the United Kingdom in 1993

1 3 5 7 9 10 8 6 4 2

© 1963 Arnoldo Mondadori Editore S.p.A., Milano
English translation copyright © 1993 by
Harcourt Brace Jovanovich, Inc. and Jonathan Cape

Umberto Eco has asserted his right
under the Copyright, Designs and Patents Act, 1988
to be identified as the author of this work

First published in the United Kingdom in 1993 by
Jonathan Cape
Random House, 20 Vauxhall Bridge Road, London SW1V 2SA

Random House Australia (Pty) Limited
20 Alfred Street, Milsons Point, Sydney,
New South Wales 2061, Australia

Random House New Zealand Limited
18 Poland Road, Glenfield,
Auckland 10, New Zealand

Random House South Africa (Pty) Limited
PO Box 337, Bergvlei, South Africa

Random House UK Limited Reg. No. 954009

A CIP catalogue record for this book
is available from the British Library

ISBN 0–224–03069–8

Printed and bound in Great Britain by
Mackays of Chatham PLC, Chatham, Kent

Contents

Music-hall, not poetry, is a criticism of life.

—*James Joyce*

Preface

In 1959, for *Il Verri*, a literary magazine whose contributors comprised many of the writers later to form the "Gruppo 63," I began writing a monthly column entitled *Diario minimo*, a title dictated as much by prudence as modesty. Into a publication filled with linguistic experiments of the neo-avant-garde and impressive essays on Ezra Pound and Chinese ideograms, I was introducing pages of free-wheeling reflections on some minor subjects that, often, were meant to parody the writings of other contributors to the magazine, more zealous than I. So, right at the outset, I wanted to apologize to the readers for having written those pages, pages deliberately comic and grotesque, and therefore less dignified than the rest of the magazine.

The first texts, whether by me or by my friends, from the point of view of literary genre resembled the *Mythologies* of Roland Barthes. Barthes' book had appeared in 1957, but at the time I began writing for *Diario minimo* I was not yet acquainted with it.

Otherwise I would never have dared devote, in 1960, an essay to striptease. And, I believe, it was after reading Barthes that, out of humility, I abandoned the *Mythologies* style and moved on, gradually, to pastiche.

I had a further, deeper reason for adopting pastiche: If the work of the neo-avant-garde consisted in turning inside out the languages of daily life and of literature, the comic and the grotesque should be a part of that program. The tradition of pastiche— which in France could boast such illustrious practitioners as Proust, Queneau, and the Oulipo group— had been generally less fortunate in Italian literature.

Hence the presence of *Diario minimo* in the pages of *Il Verri*. Later, in 1963, when the pieces I had published in the magazine were collected in a volume, it was given the same title, even though the contents were not a diary in the accepted sense. That volume went through several editions, and now serves as the basis for this English-language version. Since a literal translation of the title, *Minimal Diary*, would be meaningless, I have preferred to call it *Misreadings*.

Parody, like all comic writing, is linked to space and time. The tragic stories of Oedipus and of Antigone move us still, but if we lack a knowledge of classic Athens, we will be baffled by many of the allusions in Aristophanes. I apologize for employing such eminent examples, but it is easier to make my point through them.

Though the contents of this volume represent a choice, and though a couple of the most "Italian" pieces have been omitted, I feel I owe the foreign reader a few words of explanation. Explaining a joke inevitably kills its effect; but—*si parva licet componere magnis*—many of Panurge's words remain incomprehensible without a footnote explaining that his was the language of the Sorbonne.

"Granita" was meant as a parody of Nabokov's *Lolita,* exploiting also the fact that the translation of the protagonist's name is Umberto Umberto. Of course, my piece is not so much a parody of Nabokov as of the Italian translation of his novel; but what I wrote, even translated from Italian, is still readable, I think. The parody is set in the small towns of Piedmont, the region where I was born.

In "Fragments," obviously, I used the words of Italian popular songs, which in the translation have been replaced by American equivalents. In the final quotation, however, Shakespeare and Italian songs mix (in the original, instead of Shakespeare I used D'Annunzio).

As my translator indicates in a prefatory note, Mike Bongiorno, while unknown to non-Italians, belongs to a familiar, international category; and, personally, I continue to consider him a genius.

Obviously *"Esquisse d'un nouveau chat"* refers to Alain Robbe-Grillet and the *nouveau roman.* As in other instances, the parody here is meant as a tribute.

"The Latest from Heaven" reports from the next world in terms of current political jargon. It was written several decades ago, but I think it will be comprehensible also in the age of Ross Perot and Pat Buchanan.

The classics of Anglo-Saxon anthropology (Margaret Mead, Ruth Benedict, Kroeber, etc.) were the inspiration for "Industry and Sexual Repression in a Po Valley Society," the title borrowed from a work by Malinowski. Its philosophical parts are enhanced by some quotations (suitably modified) from Husserl, Binswanger, Heidegger, and others. The Porta Ludovica paradox has become, in Italy, a set subject for study in the architecture departments of several universities.

In the same vein, "The End Is at Hand" is inspired by the social criticism of Adorno and the school of Frankfurt. Certain passages are indirect quotations from Italian authors who were given to "Adornizing" in those years. Like the piece that precedes it, this text is an exercise in what is called today "alternative anthropology" (not the world of others as seen by us, but our world as seen by others). Montesquieu already did this with *Les Lettres Persanes.* Some time ago, a group of anthropologists invited African researchers to France so that they could observe the French way of life. The Africans were amazed to find, for example, that the French were in the habit of walking their dogs.

The TV coverage of the first moon walk suggested "The Discovery of America." In the original, the names of Italian anchormen were used; familiar American names have been substituted.

The title "My Exagmination . . ." repeats almost literally that of a famous collection of essays on *Finnegans Wake.* Bearing in mind all the critical styles in fashion at American universities a few decades ago (from New Criticism to various forms of symbolic criticism, and also a few hints at the criticism of Eliot), I adapted these attitudes of overinterpretation to the most famous Italian novel of the nineteenth century. Most English-language readers will not be familiar with *I promessi sposi* (though an English translation exists, *The Betrothed*), but it should suffice to know that my Joycean reading is applied to a classic that dates from the early nineteenth century, its style and narrative structure recalling Walter Scott (for example) more than Joyce. Today I realize that many recent exercises in "deconstructive reading" read as if inspired by my parody. This is parody's mission: it must never be afraid of going too far. If its aim is true, it simply heralds what others will later produce, unblushing, with impassive and assertive gravity.

Umberto Eco

Granita

The present manuscript was given to me by the warden of the local jail in a small town in Piedmont. The unreliable information this man furnished us about the mysterious prisoner who left these papers behind in his cell, the obscurity that shrouds the writer's fate, a widespread, inexplicable reticence in all whose paths crossed that of the author of the following pages oblige us to be content with what we know; as we must be content with what is left of the manuscript—after the voracity of the prison rats—since we feel that even in these circumstances the reader can form a notion of the extraordinary tale of this Umberto Umberto (unless the mysterious prisoner is perhaps Vladimir Nabokov, paradoxically a refugee in the Langhe region, and the manuscript shows the other face of that protean immoralist) and thus finally can draw from these pages the hidden lesson: the libertine garb conceals a higher morality.

Granita. Flower of my adolescence, torment of my nights. Will I ever see you again? Granita. Granita.

Gran-i-ta. Three syllables, the second and third forming a diminutive, as if contradicting the first. Gran. Ita. Granita, may I remember you until your image has become a shadow and your abode the grave.

My name is Umberto Umberto. When the crucial event occurred, I was submitting boldly to the triumph of adolescence. According to those who knew me then, and not those who see me now, Reader, in this cell, haggard, with the first traces of a prophet's beard stiffening my cheeks . . . according to those who knew me then, I was an ephebe of parts, with that hint of melancholy due, I believe, to the Mediterranean chromosomes of a Calabrian ancestor. The young girls I met desired me with all the violence of their burgeoning wombs, transferring me into the telluric anguish of their lonely nights. I scarcely remember those girls, as I myself was the horrible prey of quite another passion; my eyes barely grazed their cheeks gilded in the slanting sunset light by a silken, transparent down.

I loved, dear Reader, dear friend! And with the folly of my eager years, I loved those whom you would call, in your sluggish thoughtlessness, "old women." From the deepest labyrinth of my beardless being, I desired those creatures already marked by stern, implacable age, bent by the fatal rhythm of their eighty years, horribly undermined by the shadow of senescence. To denote those creatures ignored by the many, forgotten in the lubricious indifference of the customary *usagers* of sturdy Friulan milkmaids of twenty-five, I will employ, dear Reader—oppressed here again by the reflux of an intrusive knowledge that impedes, arrests any innocent act I might venture—a term that I do not despair of having chosen with precision: nornettes.

How can I describe, O you who judge me *(toi, hypocrite lecteur, mon semblable, mon frère!),* the matutinal prey offered the crafty fancier of nornettes in this swamp of our buried world? How can I convey this to you, who course through afternoon gardens in banal pursuit of maidens beginning to bud? What can you know of the subdued, shadowy, grinning hunt that the lover of nornettes may conduct on the benches of old parks, in the scented penumbra of basilicas, on the graveled paths of suburban cemeteries, in the Sunday hour at the corner of the nursing home, at the doors of the hospice, in the chanting ranks of parish processions, at charity bazaars: an amorous, intense, and—alas—inexorably chaste ambush, to catch a closer glimpse of those faces furrowed by volcanic wrinkles, those eyes watering with cataract, the twitching movement of those dry lips sunken in the exquisite depression of a toothless mouth, lips enlivened at times by a glistening trickle of salivary ecstasy, those proudly gnarled hands, nervously, lustfully tremulous, provocative, as they tell a very slow rosary!

Can I ever recreate, Reader-friend, the sinking desperation on sighting that elusive prey, the spasmodic shiver at certain fleeting contacts: an elbow's nudge in a crowded tram—"Excuse me, madam, would you like a seat?" Oh, satanic friend, how dared you accept the moist look of gratitude and the

"Thank you, young man, how kind!", when you would have have preferred to enact on the spot a bacchic drama of possession?—the grazing of a venerable knee as your calf slides between two rows of seats in the pomeridian solitude of a neighborhood cinema, or the tender but controlled grasp—sporadic moments of extreme contact!—of the skeletal arm of a crone you helped cross at the light with the prim concern of an eagle scout.

The vicissitudes of my idle youth afforded me other encounters. As I have said, I had a reasonably engaging appearance, with my dark cheeks and the tender countenance of a maiden oppressed by a delicate virility. I was not unaware of adolescent love, but I submitted to it as if paying a toll, fulfilling the requirements of my age. I recall a May evening, shortly before sunset, when in the garden of a patrician villa—it was in the Varese region, not far from the lake, red in the sinking sun—I lay in the shade of some bushes with a fledgling sixteen-year-old, all freckles and powerless in the grip of a dismaying storm of amorous feelings toward me. And it was at that moment, while I was listlessly granting her the desired wand of my pubescent thaumaturgy, that I saw, Reader, at a window of the upper floor, the form of a decrepit nanny bent almost double as she unrolled down her leg the shapeless mass of a cotton stocking. The breathtaking sight of that swollen limb, with its varicose marbling, stroked by the clumsy movement of the old hands unrolling the lumpy article of clothing, seemed to me (to my concupiscent eyes!) a brutal and enviable phallus soothed by a virginal caress: and it was at that moment that, seized by an ecstasy redoubled by distance, I exploded, gasping, in an effusion of biological assent that the maiden (foolish tadpole, how I hated you!) welcomed, moaning, as a tribute to her own callow charms.

Did you then ever realize, my dull-witted instrument of redirected passion, that you had enjoyed the food of another's repast, or did the dim vanity of your unripe years portray me to you as a fiery, unforgettable accomplice in sin? After leaving the next day with your family, you sent me a week later a postal card signed "Your old friend." Did you perceive the truth, revealing to me your perspicacity in the careful employment of that adjective, or was yours simply a bravado use of jargon, the mettlesome high-school girl rebelling against correct epistolary style?

Ah, after that, how I stared, trembling, at every window in the hope of glimpsing the flaccid silhouette of an octogenarian in the bath! How many evenings, half hidden by a tree, did I consummate my solitary debauches, my eyes trained on the shadow cast against a curtain, of some grandmother sweetly engaged in gumming a meal! And the horrid disappointment, immediate and destructive *(tiens, donc, le salaud!)*, when the figure, abandoning the falsehood of those *ombres chinoises*, revealed itself at the sill for what she was, a naked ballerina with swelling breasts and the tanned hips of an Andalusian mare!

So for months and years I coursed, unsated, in the deluded hunt for adorable nornettes, caught up in a pursuit that was born, indestructible, I am sure, at the moment of my birth, when a toothless old midwife—my father's desperate search at that hour of the night had produced only this hag, with one foot in the grave!—rescued me from the viscous prison of the maternal womb and revealed to me, in the light of life, her immortal countenance: a *jeune parque.*

I seek no justification from you who read me *(à la guerre comme à la guerre);* I am merely explaining to you how inevitable was the concurrence of events that brought me to my triumph.

The soirée to which I had been invited was a sordid petting party with young models and pimply university students. The sinuous lewdness of those aroused maidens, the negligent offering of their breasts through unbuttoned blouses in the swirl of the dance, disgusted me. I was already thinking to run away from that place of banal traffic among crotches as yet intact, when a shrill, strident sound (will I ever be able to express the dizzying pitch, the hoarse descent of those vocal cords, long exhausted, the *allure suprême de ce cri centenaire?),* the tremulous lament of an ancient female, plunged the assembly into silence. And in the frame of the doorway I saw her, the face of the remote Norn of my natal shock, the cascading enthusiasm of her lasciviously white locks, the stiffened body that stretched the stuff of the little, threadbare black dress into acute angles, the legs now thin and bent opposing arcs, the fragile line of her vulnerable femur outlined under the ancient modesty of the venerable skirt.

The insipid maiden who was our hostess made a show of tolerant politeness. She raised her eyes to heaven as she said, "She's my granny . . ."

At this point the intact part of the manuscript ends. What can be inferred from the scattered lines that follow suggests that the story continued more or less in this fashion: A few days later, Umberto Umberto abducts his hostess's grandmother, carrying her off on the handlebars of his bicycle, toward Piedmont. At first he takes her to a home for the aged poor, where, that same night, he possesses her, discovering among other things that the woman is not without previous experience. At daybreak, as he is smoking a cigarette in the semidarkness of the garden, he is approached by a dubious-looking youth who asks him slyly if the old woman is really his grandmother. Alarmed, Umberto Umberto leaves the institution with Granita and begins a dizzying race over the roads of Piedmont. He visits the wine fair at Canelli, the annual truffle festival at Alba, participates in the historical pageant at Caglianetto, inspects the livestock market at Nizza Monferrato, and follows the election of Miss Milkmaid in Ivrea and the sack race in honor of the patron saint's day in Condove. At the end of his mad odyssey through that northern region, he realizes that for some time his bicycle has been slyly followed by an eagle scout on a motorscooter, who eludes every attempt to trap him. One day, at Incisa Scapaccino, when he takes Granita to a chiropodist, leaving her alone for a few minutes while he goes to buy cigarettes, he discovers, on returning, that the old woman has abandoned him, running off with her new kidnapper. For several months he sinks into deep depression, but finally finds the old woman again, fresh from a beauty farm where her seducer has taken her. Her face is without a wrinkle, her hair is a coppery blond, her smile is dazzling. Umberto Umberto is overwhelmed by a profound sense of pity and a resigned despair at the sight of this destruction. Without a word, he purchases a shotgun and sets out in search of the villain. He finds the young scout at a campsite rubbing two sticks together to light a fire. He shoots once, twice, three times, repeatedly missing the youth, until finally two priests wearing leather jackets and black berets overpower him. Promptly arrested, he is sentenced to six months for illegal possession of firearms and hunting out of season.

1959

Fragments

_____

Proceedings, IV Intergalactic Congress of Archeological Studies, Sirius, 4th section, Mathematical Year 121. Paper read by chair Prof. Anouk Ooma of the Department of Archeology, Prince Joseph's Land University, Arctica, Earth.

Distinguished colleagues,

You are surely not unaware that for some time Arctic scholars have been engaged in intense research and have, as a result, brought to light numerous relics of the ancient civilization that flourished in the temperate and tropical zones of our planet before the catastrophe of the year then known as 1980, in the ancient era, or, more correctly, Year One, after the Explosion destroyed every trace of life in those zones. For millennia afterward, as everyone knows, they remained so contaminated by radioactivity that until a few decades ago our expeditions could approach these territories only at extreme risk, despite the eagerness of scientists to reveal to the whole Galaxy the degree of civilization achieved by our remote ancestors. One mystery will always remain with us: How could human beings inhabit areas so unbearably torrid, and how could they adapt to the insane way of living necessitated by the alternation of brief periods of light with equally brief periods of darkness? And yet we know that the ancient earthlings, in that blinding vertigo of obscurity and clarity, managed to establish efficient biorhythms and develop a rich and articulate civilization. About seventy years ago (to be precise, in the year 1745 post explosion), from the advanced base at Reykjavik, the legendary southernmost point of terrestrial life, an expedition led by Professor Amaa A. Kroak advanced as far as the desert once known as France. There, that unparalleled scholar proved beyond the shadow of a doubt that the combined effects of radioaction and time had destroyed all fossil evidence. There seemed no hope, then, that anything would ever be known about our distant progenitors. Previously, in 1710 P.E., the expedition led by Professor Ulak Amjacoa, thanks to generous support provided by the Alpha Centauri Foundation, had taken soundings in the radioactive waters of Loch Ness and recovered what is today generally considered the first "cryptolibrary" of the ancients. Encased in an enormous block of cement was a zinc container with the words incised on it: BERTRANDUS RUSSELL SUBMERSIT ANNO HOMINIS MCMLI. This container, as all of you know, held the volumes of the Encyclopaedia Britannica, and finally supplied us with that enormous body of data about the vanished civilization that have, to a great extent, formed the basis of our present historical knowledge. It was not long before other cryptolibraries were discovered in other areas (including the famous one in a sealed case in the Deutschland Territory with the inscription TENEBRA APPROPINQUANTE). It soon became clear that among the ancient earthlings only men of culture sensed the approaching tragedy. They tried to offer some remedy in the only way available to them: that is, saving for posterity the treasures of their civilization. And what an act of faith it was, for them to foresee, despite all evidence to the contrary, any posterity at all!

Thanks to these pages, which we cannot regard without emotion today, distinguished colleagues, at last we are able to know how that world thought, how its people acted, how the final drama unfolded. Oh, I realize full well that the written word provides an inadequate testimony of the world in which it was written, but think how handicapped we are when we lack even this valuable aid! The "Italian problem" offers us a typical example of the enigma that has fascinated archeologists and historians, none of whom has yet been able to give an answer to the familiar question: Why, in that country, the seat of an ancient civilization, as we know and as books discovered in other lands amply demonstrate—why, we ask, has it been impossible to find any trace of a cryptolibrary? You know that the hypotheses forwarded in answer to this question are as numerous as they are unsatisfactory; but at the risk of repeating what you already know, I will list them for you briefly:

1) The Aakon-Sturg Hypothesis, proposed with admirable erudition in *The Explosion in the Mediterranean Basin*, Baffin, 1750 P.E. A combination of thermonuclear phenomena destroyed the Italian cryptolibrary. This hypothesis is supported by sound argument, because we know that the Italian peninsula was the most heavily hit when the first atomic missiles were fired from the Adriatic coast, initiating the total conflict.

2) The Ugum-Noa Noa Hypothesis, expounded in the widely read *Did Italy Exist?* (Barents City, 1712 P.E.). Here, on the basis of careful examination of the reports of high-level political conferences held before the total conflict, the author reaches the conclusion that "Italy" never existed. While this hypothesis neatly resolves the problem of cryptolibraries (or, rather, of their absence), it seems contradicted by a series of reports provided in the English and German languages concerning the culture of the "Italian" people. Documents in the French language, on the other hand, Ugum-Noa Noa reminds us, ignore the subject altogether, thus lending some support to his bold idea.

3) The Hypothesis of Professor Ixptt Adonis (cf. *Italia*, Altair, 22nd section, Mathematical Year 120). This is without doubt the most brilliant hypothesis of all, but also the least substantiated. It argues that at the time of the Explosion the Italian National Library was, for unspecified reasons, in a state of extreme disarray; that Italian scholars, rather than concern themselves with establishing libraries for the

future, were seriously worried about their library of the present, having to make enormous efforts just to prevent the collapse of the building that actually housed the volumes. This hypothesis betrays the ingenuousness of a modern, non-earthling observer quick to weave a halo of legend around everything regarding our planet, accustomed to considering earthlings as a people who lived in idle bliss, gorging on seal pie and strumming reindeer-horn harps. On the contrary, the advanced degree of civilization reached by the ancient earthlings before the Explosion makes such criminal neglect inconceivable, the more so since exploration of the other cisequatorial countries has revealed the existence of quite advanced techniques of book conservation.

And so we come full circle. The darkest mystery has always enshrouded Italian pre-Explosion culture, even though for the early centuries the cryptolibraries of other countries supply adequate documentation. True, in the course of careful excavation some interesting if puzzling documents, highly fragile, have been discovered. I will cite here the small paper fragment unearthed by Kosamba. Its text, he rightly considers, illustrates the Italian taste for brief and pithy poems. I quote the text in its entirety: "In the middle of the pathway of this our life." Kosamba also found the jacket of a volume, obviously a treatise on horticulture, entitled *The Name of the Rose,* by a certain Ache or Eke (the upper part of the relic is unfortunately torn, so the exact name is uncertain, as Sturg indicates). And we must remember how

Italian science in that period had clearly made great progress in genetics, even though this knowledge was employed in racial eugenics, as we can infer from the lid of a box that must have contained a medicine for the improvement of the race, bearing only the words WHITER THAN WHITE accompanied by the letters AJAX (a reference to the first Aryan warrior).

Despite these valuable documents, no one has yet been able to form a precise picture of the spiritual level of that people, a level, if I may venture to say so, distinguished colleagues, that is fully communicated only by the poetic word, by poetry as imaginative awareness of a world and of a historical position.

If I have permitted myself this long but I hope not unhelpful preface, it is because I wish to report to you now, with great emotion, how I and my accomplished colleague Baaka B. B. Baaka A.S.P.Z. of the Royal Institute of Literature of Bear Island made an extraordinary find in a forbidding region of the Italian peninsula, at a depth of three thousand meters. Our trove was sealed fortuitously in a stream of lava and providentially sunk into the depths of the earth by the frightful upheaval of the Explosion. Worn and tattered, with many sections missing, almost illegible and yet filled with breathtaking revelations, this small book is of modest appearance and dimensions, bearing on the title page the words: *Great Hit Songs of Yesterday and Today.* (Considering the site of the discovery, we have called it *Quaternulus Pompeianus*). We all know, my dear colleagues, that the word "song" corresponds to the Italian *canzone* or *canzona,* an archaic term indicating certain poetic compositions of the ancient fourteenth century, as the Encyclopaedia Britannica confirms; and we assume that the word "hit," like the word "beat" (found elsewhere), must be associated with rhythm, a characteristic that music shares with the mathematical and genetic sciences. Among many peoples rhythm had assumed also a philosophical significance and was used to indicate a special quality of artistic structures (cf. the volume found in the Cryptobibliothèque National de Paris, M. Ghyka, *Essai sur le rhythme*, N.R.F. 1938). Our *Quaternulus* is an exquisite anthology, then, of the most worthy poetic compositions of the period, a compendium of lyric poems and songs that open to the mind's eye an unparalleled panorama of beauty and spirituality.

Poetry of the twentieth century of the ancient era, in Italy as elsewhere, was a poetry of crisis, boldly aware of the world's impending fate. At the same time, it was a poetry of faith. We have here a line— alas, the only legible one—of what must have been an ode condemning terrestrial concerns: "It's a material world." Immediately after that we are struck by the lines of another fragment, apparently from a propitiatory or fertility hymn to nature: "I'm singing in the rain, just singing in the rain, it's a glorious feeling . . ." It is easy to imagine this sung by a chorus of young girls: the delicate words evoke the image of maidens in white veils dancing at sowing time in some *pervigilium*. But elsewhere we find a sense of desperation, of clear awareness of the critical moment, as in this merciless depiction of solitude and confused identity, which, if we are to believe what the Encyclopaedia Britannica says of the dramatist Luigi Pirandello, might lead us to attribute the text to him: "Who? Stole my heart away? Who? Makes me dream all day? Who . . ." Another *canzona* ("Mine in May, his in June. She forgot me mighty soon") suggests a worthy correlative to some English verses of the same period, the song of James Prufrock by the poet Thomas Stearns, who speaks of an unspecified "cruellest month."

Did this searing anguish perhaps drive some exponents of poetry to seek refuge in the georgic or the didactic? Take, for example, the pristine beauty of this line: "A sleepy lagoon, a tropical moon . . ." Here you have the familiar and symbolic use of water imagery, then the regal and sublime presence of the moon, hinting at human frailty in the face of the mysterious immensity of nature. And I'm sure you will share my admiration for these verses: "June is bustin' out all over, all over the meadow and the plain; the corn is as high as an elephant's eye . . ." Clearly the text derives from the rites of fertility, the spirit of spring and of human sacrifice, perhaps a maiden's heart offered to the earth mother. Such rites were, in their day, analyzed in the England Region in a book of uncertain attribution usually called *The Golden Bough*, though some read the title as *The Golden Bowl* (cf. passim the study, as yet untranslated, by Axbzz Eowrrsc, "Golden Bough or Golden Bowl? Xpt Agrschh Clwoomai," Arcturus, 2nd section, Mathematical Year 120).

It is tempting to link the same fertility rites or, more precisely, the Phrygian rite of the death of

22

Atys, with another beautiful song that begins: "I
went down to the St. James Infirmary, to see my
baby there, laid out on a cold white table . . ." The
reference to Saint James suggests the Spanish San-
tiago, and a happy intuition led us to recognize this
also as the name of a celebrated pilgrimage city. We
then realized that we had come upon an uncompleted
translation of an Iberian poem. As we all are sadly
aware, no Spanish text has ever been recovered, since,
as the Encyclopaedia Britannica informs us, about
twenty years before the Explosion the religious authorities of that nation ordered the burning of all
books that did not have a particular nihil obstat. But
for some time now, thanks to brief quotations found
in foreign volumes, we have formed a fairly clear
idea of the figure of the mythic Catalan bard of the
nineteenth or twentieth century, Federico Garcia,
also identified as Federico Lorca, barbarously mur-
dered, the legend goes, by twenty-five women whom
he had coldly seduced. A German writer of 1966
(C. K. Dyroff, *Lorca: Ein Beitrag zum Duendege-
schichte als Flamencowissenschaft*) speaks of Lorca's
poetry as of a "being-in-death-rooted-like-love,
wherein the spirit of the time is named revealing itself
to itself through funereal danced cadences under an
Andalusian sky." These words, unusually suited to
the abovementioned text, allow us also to attribute
to the same author other magnificent verses, of hot
Iberian violence, printed in the *Quaternulus: "Cuando
caliente el sol su esta playa . . ."* If I may take the
liberty, dear friends, today, when spatiovision sets
are bombarding us constantly with an avalanche of

23

murky and dreadfully imitative music, today, when the irresponsible bawlers of drivel teach their children songs with absurd words, of recalling the crucial essay "The Decline of Arctic Man," which describes how an unknown bandleader actually set to music an obscene verse typical of drunken sailors ("No, I will not see it, Ignacio's blood on the sand"), the latest product of industrial nonsense. Let me now say that those immortal lines of Lorca, which reach us from the dark night of time, testify to the moral and intellectual stature of an earthling of two thousand years ago. We have before us a poem that is not based on the tortuous, labyrinthine research of an intellect bloated with culture but employs rhythms that are spontaneous and elementary, pure in their youthful grace; a poem that leads us to think that a God, not creative travail, is responsible for such a miracle. Great poetry, ladies and gentlemen, is universally recognizable; its stylemes cannot be mistaken; there are cadences that reveal their kinship even if they resound from opposite ends of the cosmos. So it is with joy and profound emotion, distinguished colleagues, that I have finally succeeded in making a scholarly collation, by placing an isolated verse found on a scrap of paper two years ago among the ruins of a Northern Italian city into the context of a more extensive song whose complete text I believe I have now assembled on the basis of two pages in the *Quaternulus*. An exquisite composition, rich in learned references, a jewel in its Alexandrine aura, perfect in its every turn of phrase:

Ciao ciao bambina
Get thee to a nunnery
Nunnery, hey nonny!
Come back to Sorrento
As dreams are made on . . .

I'm afraid the time allowed me for this paper is up. I would like to discuss the material further, but I am confident that I will be able to translate and publish, once I have solved a few delicate philological problems, the fruits of my invaluable discovery. In conclusion, I leave you with the image of this lost civilization that, dry-eyed, sang its own destruction of values, and with lighthearted elegance uttered diamond words that depicted for all time a world of grace and beauty. But with a presentiment of the end there was also a prophetic sensitivity. From the bottomless, mysterious depths of the past, from the worn and defaced pages of the *Quarternulus Pompeianus,* in one verse isolated on a page darkened by radiation we find perhaps a presage of what was to happen. On the very eve of the Explosion, the poet saw the destiny of the earth's population, which would build a new and more mature civilization on the icecap of the pole and find in Inuit stock the superior race of a renewed and happy planet. The poet saw that the way of the future would lead from the horrors of the Explosion to virtue and progress. Seeing this, he no longer felt fear or remorse, and so into his song poured out this verse, direct as a psalm:

"Button up your overcoat if you're on a spree. Take good care of yourself."

Just one verse; but to us, children of the prosperous and progressive Arctic, it comes as a message of faith and solidarity from the chasm of pain, beauty, death, and rebirth, in which we glimpse the beautiful and beloved countenance of our fathers.

1959

The Socratic Strip

When she appears on the little stage of the Crazy Horse, shielded by a black mesh curtain, Lilly Niagara is already naked. Something more than naked: she is wearing an undone black bra and a garter belt. During the first part of her number she dresses indolently, or rather, she slips on stockings, and fastens them to the casual harness that dangles over her limbs. She devotes the second part of her act to returning to the initial situation. Thus the audience, uncertain whether this woman has dressed or undressed, does not realize that practically speaking she has done nothing, because the slow, pained movements, delicately underlined by the anguish of her facial expression, simply declare her determined professionalism and faithfully follow a grand tradition now codified even in instruction manuals; and thus nothing is unexpected, nothing is seductive. Compared to the techniques of other grand mistresses of striptease, who know how to gauge accurately their offer of an introductory innocence, which they conclude with abundant, unpredictable slyness, lasciviousness kept in reserve, with savage twists for the final outrage (mistresses, in sum, of a dialectic, Occidental strip), the technique of Lilly Niagara is already *beat* and *hard*. It recalls, on sober consideration, the Cecilia of Moravia's *La noia,* a bored sexuality composed of indifference, here spiced by an expertise borne like a penance.

Lilly Niagara, then, wishes to achieve the ultimate level of striptease. She does not present the spectacle of a seduction directed at no one, that makes promises to the crowd but withdraws the offer at the last moment; rather, she crosses the final threshold and denies even the promise of seduction. So if the traditional striptease is the suggestion of a coitus that suddenly proves to be interruptus, provoking in devotees a mystique of privation, the strip of Lilly Niagara chastises the presumption of her new disciples, revealing to them that the promised reality is only to be contemplated, and that even the complete enjoyment of that contemplation is denied, for it must take place in silent immobility. Lilly Niagara's Byzantine art preserves, however, the habitual structure of conventional striptease and its symbolic nature.

It is only in some *boîtes* of the most total ill fame that at the end of the performance you can induce the performer to sell herself. At the Crazy Horse you are instructed, with the greatest urbanity, that it is not considered proper to ask to purchase photographs. What can be seen appears only for a few minutes within the magic area of the stage. And if you read the articles on stripping that enrich some of the publications on sale in the leading theaters, you realize that the nude dancer typically exercises her profession with strict diligence, dedicating herself in her private life to domestic affections, to the young fiancé who accompanies her to her job, or, totally submissive, to a jealous husband within impervious walls. Nor should this be thought merely a cheap device. In the bold and more innocent Belle Epoque, however, managers went to great lengths to convince the customers that their divas were insatiable monsters in private as in public, devourers of men and wealth, priestesses of the most unspeakable refinements in the boudoir.

But the Belle Epoque staged its sumptuous sinfulness for a well-to-do ruling class, to whom the theater and the after-theater had to bow, a class who enjoyed the total possession of objects, the inalienable privilege of money.

The striptease you can see for quite reasonable sums and at any hour of the day, even in your shirt sleeves—no dress code—and even twice, because the spectacle is nonstop, this striptease is addressed to the average citizen. And in offering him those minutes of religious concentration, its theology is implied, introduced in the form of hidden persuasion and displayed through *quaestiones*. The essence of this theology is that the faithful worshiper can admire the luxurious goods of female plenitude but cannot make use of them, because such dominion is not his to command. He can use, if he wishes, the women that society grants him and that destiny has assigned him. But a crafty notice at the Crazy Horse warns him that if, when he goes home, he finds his wife unsatisfactory, he can enroll her in the afternoon courses in deportment and mime that the management organizes for students and housewives. It is not certain such courses actually exist or that the customer would dare make such a suggestion to his better half; what matters is that the seed of doubt is planted in his mind, the suspicion that if the stripteaseuse is Woman, then his wife is something else, whereas if his wife is Woman, then the stripteaseuse must be something more, the Female Principle or sex or ecstasy or sin or glamor. She is, in any case, that which is denied him, the spectator; the basic element that eludes him, the goal of ecstasy that he cannot achieve, the sense of triumph that is arrested in him, the fullness of the senses and the dominion of the world that he knows only from hearsay. The typical striptease relationship demands that the woman, who has offered the definitive spectacle of her possibilities of satisfaction, is absolutely not for consumption. A booklet distributed at the Concert Mayol contains a wearily rakish introductory essay, which concludes, nevertheless, with a revealing intuition. It says, roughly, that the triumph of the naked woman in the spotlights, as she exposes herself to the gaze of a frustrated and yearning audience, consists of the artful awareness that at that moment they are comparing her with their familiar fare, and so her triumph consists also of the humiliation of others, while the pleasure of those who watch consists mainly of their own humiliation, felt, suffered, and accepted as the essence of the ritual.

If, psychologically speaking, the striptease relationship is sadomasochistic, sociologically this sadomasochism is essential to the educational rite that is being fulfilled. The striptease unconsciously teaches the spectator, who seeks and accepts frustration, that the means of production are not in his possession.

But if sociologically it introduces an undeniable hierarchy of caste (or, if you prefer, of class), metaphysically the striptease leads the spectator to compare the pleasures at his disposal with those that by their very nature he cannot have: his reality compared with the ideal, his women compared with Womanhood, his experience of sex compared with Sex, the nudes he possesses compared with the hyperuranian Nudity he will never know. Afterward, he will have to go back to the cave and be content with the shadows on the wall: those are granted to him. And thus, with unconscious synthesis, the striptease restores the Platonic situation to the sociological reality of oppression and other-direction.

Sustained by the fact that the command buttons of political life do not belong to him and that the pattern of his experiences is sanctioned by a realm of ideas he cannot alter, the striptease spectator can peacefully return to the responsibilities of every day, after the cathartic ritual that has confirmed his position as a fixed and solid element in the existing order; and locales less ascetic than the Crazy Horse (monastery for Zen monks, last stage of perfection) will allow him to carry away the images of what he sees there, to console his human condition with the wicked practices that his devotion and his solitude will suggest.

1960

Regretfully, We
Are Returning Your . . .
Readers' Reports

Anonymous, *The Bible*

I must say that the first few hundred pages of this manuscript really hooked me. Action-packed, they have everything today's reader wants in a good story. Sex (lots of it, including adultery, sodomy, incest), also murder, war, massacres, and so on.

The Sodom and Gomorrah chapter, with the transvestites putting the make on the angels, is worthy of Rabelais; the Noah stories are pure Jules Verne; the escape from Egypt cries out to be turned into a major motion picture . . . In other words, a real blockbuster, very well structured, with plenty of twists, full of invention, with just the right amount of piety, and never lapsing into tragedy.

But as I kept on reading, I realized that this is actually an anthology, involving several writers, with many—too many—stretches of poetry, and passages that are downright mawkish and boring, and jeremiads that make no sense.

The end result is a monster omnibus. It seems to have something for everybody, but ends up appealing to nobody. And acquiring the rights from all these different authors will mean big headaches, unless the editor take cares of that himself. The editor's name, by the way, doesn't appear anywhere on the manuscript, not even in the table of contents. Is there some reason for keeping his identity a secret?

I'd suggest trying to get the rights only to the first five chapters. We're on sure ground there. Also come up with a better title. How about *The Red Sea Desperadoes?*

Homer, *The Odyssey*

Personally, I like this book. A good yarn, exciting, packed with adventure. Sufficient love interest, both marital fidelity and adulterous flings (Calypso is a great character, a real man-eater); there's even a Lolita aspect, with the teenager Nausicaa, where the author doesn't spell things out, but it's a turn-on anyway. Great dramatic moments, a one-eyed giant, cannibals, even some drugs, but nothing illegal, because as far as I know the lotus isn't on the Narcotics Bureau's list. The final scene is in the best tradition of the Western: some heavy fist-swinging, and the business with the bow is a masterstroke of suspense.

What can I say? It's a page turner, all right, not like the author's first book, which was too static, all concerned with unity of place and tediously over-plotted. By the time the reader reached the third battle and the tenth duel, he already got the idea. Remember how the Achilles-Patroclus story, with that vein of not-so-latent homosexuality, got us into trouble with the Boston authorities? But this second book is a totally different thing: it reads as smooth as silk. The tone is calmer, pondered but not ponderous. And then the montage, the use of flashbacks, the stories within stories . . . In a word, this Homer is the right stuff. He's smart.

Too smart, maybe . . . I wonder if it's all really his own work. I know, of course, a writer can improve with experience (his third book will probably be a sensation), but what makes me uncomfortable—and, finally, leads me to cast a negative vote—is the mess the question of rights will cause. I broached the subject with a friend at William Morris, and I get bad vibes.

In the first place, the author's nowhere to be found. People who knew him say it was always hard to discuss any changes to be made in the text, because he was blind as a bat, couldn't follow the manuscript, and even gave the impression he wasn't completely familiar with it. He quoted from memory, was never sure exactly what he had written, and said the typist added things. Did he really write the book or did he just sign it?

No big deal, of course. Editing has become an art, and many books are patched together in the editor's office or written by several hands (like *Mommy Dearest*) and still turn out to be bestsellers. But this second book, there is too much unclear about it. Michael says the rights don't belong to Homer, and certain aeolian bards will have to be paid off, since they are due royalties on some parts.

A literary agent who works out of Chios says the rights belong to the local rhapsodists, who virtually ghosted the book; but it's not clear whether they are active members of that island's Writers' Guild. A PR in Smyrna, on the other hand, says the rights belong exclusively to Homer, only he's dead, and therefore the city is entitled to all royalties. But Smyrna isn't the only city that makes such a claim. The impossibility of establishing if and when Homer died means we can't invoke the '43 law regarding works published fifty years after the author's death. At this point a character by the name of Callinus pops up, insisting not only that he holds all rights but that, along with *The Odyssey*, we must buy a package including *Thebais*, *Epigoni*, and *The Cyprian Lays*. Apart from the fact that these aren't worth a dime, a number of experts think they're not even by Homer. And how do we market them? These people are talking big bucks now, and they're seeing how far they can push us. I tried asking Aristarchus of Samothrace for a preface; he has clout, and he's a good writer, too, and I thought maybe he could tidy the work up. But he wants to indicate, in the body of the book, what's authentic and what isn't; we end up with a critical edition and zilch sales. Better leave the whole thing to some university press that will take twenty years to produce the book, which they'll price at a couple hundred dollars a copy, and maybe a few libraries will actually buy it.

Bottom line: If we take the plunge, we're getting

ourselves into an endless legal hassle, the book will be impounded, but not like one of those sex books, which they then sell under the counter. This one will just be seized and forgotten. Maybe ten years from now Oxford will buy it for The World's Classics, but in the meantime you'll have spent your money, and it'll be a long wait before you see any of it again.

I'm really sorry, because the book's not bad. But we're publishers, not detectives. So I'd say pass.

Alighieri, Dante, *The Divine Comedy*

Alighieri is your typical Sunday writer. (In everyday life he's an active member of the pharmacists' guild.) Still, his work shows an undeniable grasp of technique and considerable narrative flair. The book, in the Florentine dialect, consists of about a hundred rhymed chapters, and much of it is interesting and readable. I particularly enjoyed the descriptions of astronomy and certain concise, provocative theological notions. The third part of the book is the best and will have the widest appeal; it involves subjects of general interest, concerns of the common reader— Salvation, the Beatific Vision, prayers to the Virgin. But the first part is obscure and self-indulgent, with passages of cheap eroticism, violence, and downright crudity. This is a big problem: I don't see how the reader will get past this first "canticle," which doesn't really add much to what has already been written about the next world in any number of moral tracts and treatises, not to mention the *Golden Legend* of Jacopo da Varagine.

But the greatest drawback is the author's choice of his local dialect (inspired no doubt by some crackpot avant-garde idea). We all know that today's Latin needs a shot in the arm—it isn't just the little literary cliques that insist on this. But there's a limit, after all, if not in the rules of language then at least to the public's ability to understand. We have seen what happened with the so-called Sicilian poets: their publisher went around on bicycle distributing the books among the various outlets, but the works ended up on the remainders counter anyway.

Further, if we publish a long poem in Florentine, we'll have to publish another in Milanese and another in Paduan: otherwise we lose our grip on the market. This is a job for small presses, chapbooks, etc. Personally I have nothing against rhyme, but quantitative metrics are still the most popular form with poetry readers, and I doubt that a normal reader could stomach this endless sequence of tercets, especially if he comes from Bologna, say, or Venice. So I think we'd do better to launch a series of really popular titles at reasonable prices: the works of Gildas or Anselm of Aosta, for example. And leave to the little avant-garde magazines the numbered editions on handmade paper. "For there neid faere, naenig uuirthit . . ." The linguistic hash of the postmoderns.

Tasso, Torquato, *Jerusalem Liberated*

As a "modern" epic of chivalry, this isn't bad. It's written gracefully, and the situations are fairly fresh:

high time poets stopped imitating the Breton or Carolingian cycles. But let's face it, the story is about the Crusaders and the taking of Jerusalem, a religious subject. We can't expect to sell such a book to the younger generation of "angries." At best we'll get good reviews in *Our Sunday Visitor* or maybe *The Tablet*. Even there, I have doubts about the reception of certain erotic scenes that are a bit too lewd. So my vote would be "yes," provided the author revises the work, turning it into something even nuns could read. I've already mentioned this to him, and he didn't balk at the idea of such a rewrite.

Diderot, Denis, *Les bijoux indiscrets* and *La Moine*

I confess I haven't unwrapped these two manuscripts, but I believe a reader should sense immediately what's worth devoting time to and what isn't. I know this Diderot; he makes encyclopedias (he once did some proofreading for us), and he's involved in some dreary enterprise in God knows how many volumes which will probably never see the light of day. He goes around looking for draftsmen to draw the works of a clock for him or the threads of a Gobelin tapestry, and he'll surely bankrupt his publisher. The man's a snail, and I don't really think he's capable of writing anything amusing in the fiction field, especially for a series like ours, which has some juicy, spicy little things like Restif de la Bretonne. As the old saying goes, he should stick to his last.

Sade, D. A. François, *Justine*

The manuscript was in a whole pile of things I had to look at this week and, to be honest, I haven't read it through. I opened it at random three times, in three different places, which, as you know, is enough for a trained eye.

Well, the first time I found an avalanche of words, page after page, about the philosophy of nature, with digressions on the cruelty of the struggle for survival, the reproduction of plants, and the cycles of animal species. The second time: at least fifteen pages on the concept of pleasure, the senses and the imagination, and so on. The third time: twenty pages on the question of submission between men and women in various countries of the world . . . I think that's enough. We're not looking for a work of philosophy. Today's audience wants sex, sex, and more sex. In every shape and form. The line we should follow is *Les Amours du Chevalier de Faublas*. Let's leave the highbrow stuff to Indiana.

Cervantes, Miguel, *Don Quixote*

The book—the readable parts of it, anyway—tells the story of a Spanish gentleman and his man-servant who roam the world pursuing chivalrous dreams. This Don Quixote is half crazy (the character is fully developed, and Cervantes knows how to spin a tale). The servant is a simpleton endowed with some rough common sense, and the reader identifies with him as he tries to deflate his master's fantasies.

So much for the story, which has some good dramatic twists and a number of amusing and meaty scenes. My objection is not based on my personal response to the book.

In our successful low-price series, "The Facts of Life," we have published, with admirable results, *Amadis of Gaul, The Legend of the Graal, The Romance of Tristan, The Lay of the Little Bird, The Tale of Troy,* and *Erec and Enid.* Now we also have an option on *The Kings of France* by that promising young Barberino, and if you ask me, it'll be the book of the year and maybe even a book of the month, because it has real grass-roots appeal. Now, if we do this Cervantes, we'll be bringing out a book that, for all its intrinsic value, will mess up our whole list, because it suggests those novels are lunatic ravings. Yes, I know all about freedom of expression, political correctness, and what have you, but we can't very well bite the hand that feeds us. Besides, this book seems a one-shot deal. The writer has just got out of jail, he's in bad shape, I can't remember whether it was his arm or his leg they cut off, but he certainly isn't raring to write something else. I'm afraid that in rushing to produce something new at all costs we might jeopardize a publishing program that has so far proved popular, moral, and (let's be frank) profitable. I say no.

Manzoni, Alessandro, *I Promessi sposi*

These days the blockbuster novel is apparently the rage, if you have any faith in print-run figures. But there are novels and there are novels. If we had bought Doyle's *The White Company* or Henty's *By Pike and Dyke*, at this point we'd know what to put in our paperback line. These are books people read and will be reading two hundred years from now, because they tug at the heart, are written in simple and appealing language, don't try to hide their regional origin, and they deal with contemporary themes like feudal unrest and the freedom of the Low Countries. Manzoni, on the contrary, sets his novel in the seventeenth century, a period that is a notorious turn-off. Moreover, he engages in a very dubious linguistic experiment, inventing a kind of Milanese-Florentine language that is neither fish nor fowl. I certainly wouldn't recommend it as a model for young creative-writing students. But that's not the worst. The fact is that our author sets up a lowbrow story, the tale of a poor engaged couple whose marriage is prevented by the conniving of some local overlord. In the end they do get married and everybody's happy. A bit thin, considering that the reader has to digest six hundred pages. Further, while ostensibly delivering an unctuous sermon on Providence, Manzoni actually unloads whole bundles of pessimism on us (he's a Jansenist, to call him by his right name). He addresses the most melancholy reflections on human weakness and national failings to today's public, who want something quite different, more heroic yarns, not a narrative constantly interrupted to allow the author to spout cheap philosophy or, worse, to paste together a linguistic collage, setting two seventeenth-century edicts between a dialogue half in

Latin and adding pseudo-folk talk that is hardly proper for the positive heroes the public is eager for. Having just finished that fluent and flavorsome little book, Hewlett's *The Forest Lovers,* I read this *Promessi sposi* with considerable effort. You only have to turn to page one to see how long it takes the author to get to the point. He starts with a landscape description whose syntax is so dense and labyrinthine that you can't figure out what he's saying, when it would have been so much easier to write, "One morning, in the Lecco area . . ." Well, so it goes: not everybody has the narrative gift, and even fewer have the ability to write in good Italian.

Still, the book is not totally without merit. But I warn you: it would take forever to sell out a first printing.

Proust, Marcel,
*A la recherche
du temps perdu*

This is undoubtedly a serious work, perhaps too long, but as a paperback series it could sell.

But it won't do as is. It needs serious editing. For example, the punctuation has to be redone. The sentences are too labored; some take up a whole page. With plenty of good in-house work, reducing each sentence to a maximum of two or three lines, breaking up paragraphs, indenting more often, the book would be enormously improved.

If the author doesn't agree, then forget it. As it

stands, the book is too—what's the word?—asth-matic.

Kant, Immanuel, *Critique of Practical Reason*

I asked Susan to take a look at this, and she tells me that after Barthes there's no point translating this Kant. In any case, I glanced at it myself. A reasonably short book on morality could fit nicely into our philosophy series, and might even be adopted by some universities. But the German publisher says that if we take this one, we have to commit ourselves not only to the author's previous book, which is an immense thing in at least two volumes, but also to the one he is working on now, about art or about judgment, I'm not sure which. All three books have more or less the same title, so they would have to be sold boxed (and at a price no reader could afford); otherwise bookshop browsers would mistake one for the other and think, "I've already read this." Remember the *Summa* of that Dominican? We began to translate it, and then we had to pass the rights on to Sheed and Ward because it ran way over budget.

There's another problem. The German agent tells me that we would also have to publish the minor works of this Kant, a whole pile of stuff including something about astronomy. Day before yesterday I tried to phone him directly in Koenigsberg, to see if we could do just one book, but the cleaning woman said the master was out and I should never call between five and six because that's when he takes his walk, or between three and four because that's nap time, and so on. I would advise against getting involved with a man like this: we'll end up with a mountain of his books in the warehouse.

Kafka, Franz, *The Trial*

Nice little book. A thriller with some Hitchcock touches. The final murder, for example. It could have an audience.

But apparently the author wrote under a regime with heavy censorship. Otherwise, why all these vague references, this trick of not giving names to people or places? And why is the protagonist being put on trial? If we clarify these points and make the setting more concrete (facts are needed: facts, facts, facts), then the action will be easier to follow and suspense is assured.

These young writers believe they can be "poetic" by saying "a man" instead of "Mr. So-and-so in such-and-such a city." Genuine writing has to keep in mind the old newspaper man's five questions: Who? What? When? Where? Why? If we can have a free hand with editing, I'd say buy it. If not, not.

Joyce, James, *Finnegans Wake*

Please, tell the office manager to be more careful when he sends books out to be read. I'm the English-language reader, and you've sent me a book written in some other, godforsaken language. I'm returning it under separate cover.

1972

Esquisse d'un nouveau chat

Count six paces from the corner of the room to the table. From the table to the rear wall, five paces. There is an open door opposite the table. From the door to your corner, six paces. If you look ahead, your gaze crossing the room diagonally toward the opposite corner, when you are crouched against the wall, your mask to the room, your curved tail brushing both walls where they meet to form the corner, you will then see, six paces before you, at the level of your eyes, a cylindrical form, shiny, dark brown, carved in a series of fine furrows with a whitish line in the cleft. A peeling surface about five centimeters from the ground spreads in an irregular circumference, tending to an imprecise polygon, its maximum diameter six centimeters. It has a base, also whitish, but a dimmer white than that of the furrows, as if the dust had settled there for a longer period and at a greater rate over the days or months, centuries or millennia. Over the peeling surface the cylinder rises, its shiny brown still marked by furrows, until, at a median height of one hundred twenty centimeters from the ground, it ends, surmounted by a much larger form, apparently rectangular, although your eye, beholding the object along the diagonal that runs from your corner to the corner opposite, sees it as a rhomboid. And now, extending your field of vision, you discern three other cylindrical bodies arranged in symmetry with one another and all symmetrical with respect to the first, so that they seem the three vertices of another rhomboid, and therefore if they all support, as you believe they do, the large rectangular object at one hundred twenty centimeters from the ground, they are probably positioned also at the four corners of a perfect rectangle.

Your gaze does not see precisely what is resting on the rectangular surface. From it, in your direction, a reddish mass protrudes, its entire width surrounded by a whitish material. The reddish mass rests on a yellow, wrinkled sheet of paper dotted with red at several points, as if the mass were something live that has left part of its vital humor on that rough yellow surface.

You, who have constantly before your pupil the filiform and confused curtain of the hairs of your brow, which descend to protect the almond-shaped eyeball, and, farther, as if in perspective, the imperceptibly vibrating long whiskers, now suddenly and obliquely see beneath your nose a red and wrinkled mobile surface, a brighter red than the red of the mass that rests on the rectangle.

Now you lick your whiskers at the lure of the large reddish mass; now the reddish mass, prompted by your gaze, lets fall drops of humoral liquid on the crinkly yellow sheet; now both you and the reddish mass participate in a reciprocal attraction. It is futile for you to be hypocritical: once again you are staring at the meat on the table.

So you are about to make a leap that will enable you to take possession of the meat. From the epicenter of your leap to the surface of the table is six paces; but if you turn your gaze again to the table leg, you will now see, beside it, two other tubular surfaces, also brown but less solid in appearance, more fluctuating. Now you become aware of the presence of a complementary entity that is not the table and not the meat. Below this entity you note at ground level a pair of vaguely ovoid brown shapes, the upper surface breached by a broad gap whose lips are connected by a pattern of strings, also brown. Now you know him. He is beside the table, he is beside the meat. You do not leap.

You ask yourself if you have not been in this situation once before, and if you have not witnessed a similar scene in the large picture that decorates the wall opposite the table. The picture shows a crowded tavern with a child in the corner; in the center there is a table with a big piece of meat on it, and beside the table the figure of a soldier is visible, erect, wearing loose, flapping trousers and brown shoes. In the far corner a cat can be seen preparing to leap. If you take a closer look at the picture, you will discern, in the cat's pupil, the image of an almost empty room, in whose center stands a table with cylindrical legs, and on it is a large piece of meat on a sheet of butcher's paper, yellow and rough, stained here and there with the meat's bloody traces. There is no one beside the table.

Suddenly the cat that appears in the clear reflection of the pupil of the cat in the picture makes a leap toward the meat; but at the same time the man beside the table in the picture grabs at the cat, and now you do not know if the cat that flees is the cat reflected in the pupil of the cat in the picture or if, instead, it is the cat in the picture. Probably it is you, who now flee with the meat in your mouth after you have made the leap. The one chasing you is the child who was standing in the corner of the tavern, diagonally opposite the cat in the picture.

From your eyes to the table it is five paces; from the table to the far wall, six paces; from the wall to the door, eight paces. On the table the large reddish mass of meat, still intact, cannot be seen. On the table in the picture the meat is still visible, but beside the table now you see two men in baggy brown trousers. In the corner opposite the cat in the picture the child can no longer be seen. In the reflection of the pupil of the cat in the picture you no longer see the cat in the corner, five paces from the table. This is not reality.

You would seek desperately an eraser to rub out this memory. Your tail drags in a slovenly way against the ninety-degree angle formed by the two walls that meet behind your back. You ask yourself if it is your feline condition that leads you to see the world in this objective way, or if the maze in which you find yourself is your habitual space and also the maze of the man beside the table. Or if you both are only the image in the eye above you, which subjects you both to this tension as a purely literary exercise. If that is the case, it is not fair. There should be a relationship that will allow you to unify the things that you have witnessed, the things that have witnessed you, and the things you have been. The things in which you have seen yourself motionless must have some ambiguous connection with both the things that have been seen and with you who have seen. If the man made a leap toward the picture and gripped the child with his teeth, you then pursued him into the picture, beyond the door of the tavern and into the road over which whitish flakes of snow flutter, first slanting then increasingly straight and closer to your eyes, like filiform, darting shadows, vague dots that vibrate before you. They are your whiskers. If the man took the meat, if you made your leap, if the meat was on the table, and the child fled among the flakes of snow, who has taken the meat that you will devour and that now remains on the table where you did not see it?

But you are a cat, probably, and you remain an object in this situation. You cannot alter it. You want the situation altered, but that would mean an alteration of yourself. This is your universe. What you are contemplating is a human universe of which you know nothing, just as They know nothing of yours. Still, the idea tempts you.

You contemplate a possible new novel, with yours as the ordering mind, but you do not dare carry this further, because you would inevitably introduce the horrible disorder of the evident into the tranquil improbability of your maze.

You consider the story of a cat, a respectable cat of noble birth, whom no one would expect so many and such dreadful adventures to befall, though in fact they do. This cat suffers various vicissitudes and surprises, unexpected agnitions (he has lain with his own mother, or killed his own father to gain possession of the large red chunk of meat), and as these trials multiply, the audience of cats witnessing the play feels pity and terror; until the logical development of events culminates in a sudden catastrophe, a final denouement of all tensions, after which the cats present, and you who have ordered their emotions, enjoy a purification, a catharsis.

Now you know that such a resolution would make you master of the room, and of the meat, and perhaps of the man and the child. No denials: you are morbidly drawn by this path for a future cat. But then you would be tagged a member of the avant-garde. You know you will never write this story. You have never even considered it, never told anyone you might have considered it while watching a piece of meat. You have never crouched in the corner of this room.

Now a cat is in the corner of the room where the walls meet to form a ninety-degree angle. From the tip of his whiskers to the table it is five paces.

1961

The Latest from Heaven

The passages that follow are taken from the notebook of the reporter John Smith, whose lifeless body was found on the slopes of Mount Ararat. The newspaper that employed Smith confirms that he was sent to Asia Minor on a special assignment, but refuses to disclose the nature of that assignment. Since Ararat is on the Armenian frontier, the media blackout was probably imposed by the State Department, anxious to avoid an international incident. Smith's body showed no wound beyond some severe burns, "like he'd been struck by lightning," to quote the shepherd who found him. But the Erzurum Meteorological Bureau informs us that for the past six months the area has had no storms of any kind, not even heavy rains. This text evidently represents a series of statements made to Smith by an unidentified source not named elsewhere in the notebook.

Rain! It's this damn government! You see? That cloud over there. It never stops dripping. But just try complaining. There must be more than a hundred of them around here. They spend a fortune to set up those big picturesque cirrus. Public relations, they say. While everything's going to pot around here, falling apart. Look, I'm telling you these things, but don't put down my name: I'm not asking for trouble. Besides, I'm the lowest rung on this ladder. I've been here two thousand years, but I arrived with that whole batch of Christian Martyrs, and they treat us like dogs. It's no merit of yours, they say, you have the lions to thank. You know what I mean? Except for the Holy Innocents, we're really the bottom of the heap. But what I'm saying now you can hear from ten thousand times ten thousand others, even higher up, because discontent has spread everywhere. So write it down, write it down.

Falling apart, I say. This huge bureaucracy, but nothing solid, concrete. That's the story.

And He doesn't know. Not one thing. It's all run by the Higher Echelons; their word is law, and they never let us in on anything. The machine just keeps cranking along.

You want to know something? Even today anyone who's killed ten Moslems can get in automatically: it's a rule that dates back to the First Crusade and nobody's ever bothered to repeal it. So every day twenty, thirty parachute troops come marching in, and nobody lifts a finger. I'm telling you. And there's still a Bureau for the Elimination of the Albigenses. There's no knowing what goes on there, but it exists, with its own letterhead and all the special benefits.

Try doing something about it. The Dominations—they're a terrible clique—won't let anybody get a foot in the door. Big or little, all requests get the same treatment. Consider the fuss raised over the rehabilitation of Satan. Easy enough, wouldn't you think? You open a communicating passage below, and the whole problem of evil is settled. Actually, this is what the young Thrones are after, but you see how they've been shut up. And the Guardians? Have you read about that? They were far down, very close to humans; they understood them, and naturally took their part. Well, some Guardians may have gone too far in fraternizing; class solidarity, it's only natural. So? Off they went, reassigned to the Boiler Room of the Primum Mobile. And nobody knows—I repeat, nobody!—if He was told anything. They do as they like, issuing their decrees and their letters, and nothing budges. Not an inch.

Look how many centuries it took them to accept the Ptolemaic reform. When Ptolemy died, they still hadn't ratified the Pythagorean reform, holding on to that barbaric model with the Earth flat as a dish and the edge of the abyss right beyond the Pillars of Hercules. And you know something else? When Dante arrived here, they were barely finishing with Ptolemy, there was still a Music of the Spheres Department—they hadn't realized that if each planet in its revolutions made a different sound of the scale, then all together they'd be like a kitten on the keyboard, one hell of a racket. Pardon the expression. I meant to say: infernal din.

And another thing. Just listen to this: When Galileo published the *Saggiatore*, here they were still circulating a pamphlet denouncing the Counterearth of Pythagoras. But He never heard the story of the Counterearth—I know this from a thoroughly reliable source. Throughout the entire Middle Ages He was kept in ignorance; the Seraphim gang worked hand-in-glove with the Theology Faculty in Paris, and they took charge of the whole question.

In the old Eden days He was a different being. He was something to be seen, they say! He rose in person, descended upon Adam and Eve, and you should have heard Him! And earlier still? Totally self-made, He is, with His own hands. That talk about resting on the seventh day? Ha! That's when He did His filing.

But even then, yes, even then . . . To put His hands on Chaos, what He had to go through! There was Raphael and another ten or twelve bigwigs who were opposed; they had inherited Chaos, which was then divided into estates. It was their reward for driving out the Rebels . . . So He had to use force! You should have seen Him! Moving on the face of the waters and all that: like the cavalry arriving in an old Western. Nobody who saw it has ever forgotten. Ah, the good old days.

The Rebels, you ask? Well, you know how these things go. There's the Official History now, so there's just one version, the Choirs', but as far as the truth is concerned . . . They've turned Lucifer into a premature anti-Fascist, a crypto-Communist. At most he was a Social Democrat. An intellectual with ideas about reform, that's what he was, the kind who always gets killed in revolutions. What did Lucifer want, actually? A broader representation, and the fair division of Chaos. And wasn't He then the very one who then divided up Chaos? You see how it goes, He catches on Himself finally, but nothing must be said to Him directly. Enlightened, oh yes, He's that, to be sure; but paternalistic, first and foremost.

Representation, on the other hand, is still far in the future, and that's where it'll stay. I think He'd favor change. But the Higher Orders, they whisper in his ear. Just look at what's happening with this Relativity. Would issuing a decree be all that much trouble? He knows that the space-time observations made in the Crystalline are different from those made in the Sky of Mercury. You know what I mean? Of course He knows. He made the Universe, right? But try saying so. They'll send you straight to the Primum Mobile Boiler Room. There's no way out: Once He admits the expanding universe and curved space, He'll have to abolish the departments of the Heavens and replace the Primum Mobile with a constant and diffused energy source. And then all the positions and posts will be superfluous: the Powers of the Sky of Venus, the Central Cherubinium for Firmament Maintenance, the Chief Executive Officers of the Heavens, the Seraphic Foundation of the Primum Mobile, and the Wardens of the Mystic Rose! You see what I mean? The old organization is out and a new decentralized staff chart has to be established. Ten big Archangels without portfolio: that's what'll happen. In other words, nothing will happen.

Just drop by the Primum Mobile control room

and try mentioning $E = mc^2$. They'll put you on trial for sabotage. Do you realize that the directors of the Boiler Room are still trained from a textbook written by Albert of Saxony, *The Theory and Practice of Impetus*, and the *Handy Guide to the Vis Movendi* commissioned by Buridan?

And this is where the mixups come from. Only yesterday the Bureau of Planetary Initiative set up a system near the Nebula of the Swan. You should have heard them. They talked about a stabilization of the epicycle. Well, a nova exploded that they'll remember for a millennium. The whole zone radioactive. And try to find out who's responsible. An accident, they say. But an accident means Chance, you know, and Chance means casting doubt on the Old Man's power. These are hardly trifling matters, and He knows it. He's very alert to such things. He personally wrote a memo to the joint Seven Heavens on the subversive theory of the statistics of Chance.

What can be done, you ask? Why, with radical reorganization and a new expanding structure everything can be worked out. You expand and expand, and one fine day you incorporate Hell again. And that's what they say they all want. Harmony, celestial harmony, all-embracing Love. You should hear them. But it's only talk. Gabriel, in his Jupiter address, spoke about our Heaven First policy. If you take a closer look, it means a contracting universe. Gabriel! What a character! If he could, he'd declare Earth out of bounds, like Hell. He's never been able to bear Earth. He handled the Annunciation, but his teeth were clenched the whole time. He could hardly refuse. If you only knew what he went around saying afterward, about that girl . . . For him, the Son is too far to the left. You follow me? And he's never forgiven the Paraclete for Pentecost. Those twelve guys were already too smart, he says, all they needed was the gift of tongues!

He's tough, and a demagogue. Hand-in-glove with Moses. For Gabriel, the aim of creation was the freeing of the chosen people from bondage in Egypt. Now we've done it, he says, so that's that. We should shut down the firm: it's not bringing in anything. If it weren't for the Son, by now Gabriel would have pulled it off.

You might say: Well, let's back the Son, and at the right moment he will make his move. But it's risky. The Old Man is smarter than they think, and He never forgives. And the idea of another fall of the angels scares everybody in this place. I mean everybody. Then there's the Ghost, he blows where he lists, the saying goes, so you never know what side he's on. Maybe when the right moment comes, he'll back out, and then where are we?

The Son, too . . . let me tell you. He's left-wing, true enough. Everybody's to the left, to hear them talk. But do you think he'd accept—for example— the uncertainty principle? "If you like, you can establish the position of an electron, its energy, and even the year of its birth! Just watch me!" Doesn't he realize that for others it's not so easy? But to him this is all intellectuals' hot air: "The present state of the Heavens," he said in his Christmas message this year, "represents the best organizational plan with which the Kingdom can advance toward the future while preserving respect for tradition: in short, progress without risk!" You get it?

This may all seem nonsense to you. The Earth goes ahead on its own, anyway; these characters quarrel among themselves, but nobody lays a finger on Earth for fear somebody else will want to get into the act. For us, however, it's a vital question. Those who live on the colony planets are virtually excluded from the Kingdom. And if not excluded, they have to go through torments, apply for citizenship in one of the Heavens—and then, forget it. You know: all day dancing in a ring and the only news you get is from the Blessed Vision. Yes, the one that extends all over the universe. What the Choirs want to be seen, what the Archangelic Union passes off as the Blessed Vision, that's all they see! The rest is fog. I tell you, they treat us like children.

And He knows nothing about it. He thinks of Himself thinking and therefore believes everything is fine. So they won't touch the Aristotelian model; they flatter Him with the story of the First Cause, of absolute transcendence, and they keep everything from Him.

Mind you, I'm not some kind of pantheist weirdo. Really, I'm not. I wouldn't want you to take me for a subversive or think I'm simply envious. We all agree that an Order is necessary, and He has every right to handle it. Still, He has to make some concessions. Times have changed, right?

I tell you, it can't go on like this. Too much

unrest. The people are on the move. We've come to the boiling point.

I give this another ten thousand years. Then you'll see.

1961

The Thing

───────────

"Well, Professor?" the General asked, with a hint of impatience.

"Well what?" Professor Ka said. He was clearly stalling for time.

"You've been working down here for five years, and nobody's disturbed you. We've demonstrated our faith in you. But we can't rely only on your word forever. The time has come when we must see for ourselves."

There was a threatening edge in the General's voice.

With a weary gesture, Ka smiled and said: "You catch me at my weakest moment, General. I wanted to wait a little longer, but you put me on the spot. I have made something . . ." His voice sank almost to a whisper. "Something enormous. And, by the Sun, people must know about it!"

He waved, as if to usher the General into the cave. He led him to the back, to a place illuminated by a shaft of light that entered through a narrow aperture in the wall. Here, on a smooth ledge, Ka showed him the Thing.

It was an almond-shaped object, nearly flat, its surface many-faceted, like a huge diamond, only opaque, with almost metallic glints.

"Good," the General said, puzzled. "It's a stone."

There was a sly flash in the Professor's blue eyes, beneath their bushy, bristling brows. "Yes," he said, "it's a stone. But not a stone to be left lying on the ground, among other stones. It is meant to be grasped."

"To be—?"

"Grasped, General. This stone contains all the power that man has ever dreamed of, the secret of Energy, a million manpower. Look . . ."

Cupping the palm of his hand, he crooked his fingers and placed them on the stone until he was clasping it, then raised his hand and, with it, the stone. The stone stuck to the hand, its thickest part stuck to the palm and the fingers, while the tip protruded and pointed at the ground or upward, or at the General, depending on how the Professor moved his wrist. The Professor swung his arm violently, and the tip of the stone drew a trajectory in space. The Professor brought his arm up and down, and the tip of the stone met the friable rock of the ledge. Then the wonder occurred: the tip struck the rock, penetrated it, scratched it, chipped it. As the Professor repeated this movement over and over, the tip bit the rock and made a furrow in it, then a hole, finally a crater; it wounded, it broke, it pulverized.

The General looked on wide-eyed, holding his breath. "Phenomenal!" he murmured, gulping.

"And that's nothing," the Professor said, with an expression of triumph. "Of course, striking the ledge with your hand alone, you would accomplish nothing. Now watch!" From a corner he picked up a big coconut, rough, hard, impenetrable, and handed it to the General.

"Go ahead," the Professor said. "Use both hands. Break it!"

"Oh, come now, Ka," the General said in a shaky voice. "You know very well that's impossible. None of us can do it . . . Only a dinosaur can, with a blow of his hoof. Only dinosaurs can eat the coconut's meat and drink its milk . . ."

"Well, now you can, too." The Professor's voice was filled with excitement. "Watch!"

He took the coconut and set it on the ledge, in the freshly dug crater, then grasped the stone at its opposite end, holding it now by the tip. His arm made a rapid swing, with no apparent effort, and the stone's thick bottom struck the nut, shattering it. The liquid poured onto the ledge, and bits of shell remained in the furrow, revealing the meat inside, white, cool, luscious. The General seized one of the pieces and greedily thrust it into his mouth. He looked at the stone, at Ka, at what until recently had been a coconut, and he seemed robbed of the power of speech.

"By the Sun, Ka! This is a wonderful thing. With this Thing of yours, man has multiplied his strength a hundred times. He will be able to face any dinosaur on equal terms. He's become master of rock and trees, has gained an extra arm . . . no, a hundred extra arms, an army of arms! Where did you find it?"

Ka smiled smugly. "I didn't find it. I made it."

"Made it? What do you mean?"

"I mean, it didn't exist before."

"You're crazy, Ka," the General said, quivering. "It must have fallen from the sky. An envoy of the Sun must have brought it here, a spirit of the air . . . How could anybody make what does not already exist?"

"It's possible," Ka replied calmly. "It's possible to take a stone and strike it against another stone until you've made it the shape you want. It's possible to shape it in such a way that your hand can grasp it. And with such a stone in your hand, it's possible to make many others, even bigger, sharper. I've done it, General."

The General was sweating copiously. "Why, we must tell everyone, Ka! The whole Horde must know about this. Our men will become invincible. You understand? We can take on a bear, now. A bear has claws, but we have this Thing. We can tear him to pieces before he tears us to pieces. We can stun him, kill him. We can kill a snake, crush a tortoise, kill even . . . Great Sun! . . . kill . . . another man!"

The General broke off, thunderstruck by this idea. Then he resumed speaking, with a cruel gleam in his eyes. "This way, Ka, we can attack the Koammm Horde. They are more numerous and stronger than us, but now we'll have them in our power. We'll destroy them to the last man! Ka, Ka!" The General seized the Professor by the shoulders. "Victory is ours!"

But Ka was grave, wary. He hesitated before speaking. "That's the reason I didn't want to show it to you. I realize I've made a terrible discovery. Something that will change the world. I know. I've discovered a source of frightening energy. Nothing like it has ever been seen on earth. Which is why I don't want others to know about it. With such a weapon, war would become suicide, General. The Koammm Horde would quickly learn to make it, and in the next war there would be no victors. I had conceived of this Thing as an implement of peace and progress, but now I see how dangerous it is. I'm going to destroy it."

The General was beside himself. "You're out of your mind, Ka! You've no right. You scientists and your stupid scruples! For five years you've been shut up in here and you don't know what the world is like anymore. You don't know that civilization is at a turning point. If the Koammm Horde wins, it will mean the end of peace, freedom, and joy for the human race. We have a sacred duty to possess this Thing! We won't necessarily use it, Ka. So long as everyone knows we possess it. We'll just give an experimental demonstration in the presence of our enemies. Then its use will be regulated. Nobody will dare attack us. Meanwhile, we can use it to dig graves, build new caverns, break fruit, level land. But as a weapon, we only need to possess it, not use it. It's a deterrent, Ka. It'll keep those Koammm barbarians at bay for years to come."

"No, no," Ka replied. "It must be destroyed."

"You're a bleeding-heart liberal, Ka, and also an idiot!" The General was livid. "You're playing into their hands. You're a Koammmite sympathizer, like all intellectuals, like that bard the other day who was preaching about a union of humans. You don't believe in the Sun!"

Ka shuddered. He bowed his head, his eyes narrow and sad under their bushy brows. "I knew we'd come to this. I'm no Koammmite, and you know it. But by the Fifth Rule of the Sun, I refuse to incriminate myself: it might bring down the wrath of the spirits on my head. You may think what you please, but the Thing does not leave this cavern!"

"Yes, it does, and quickly, too, for the glory of our Horde, for the sake of civilization and prosperity, and for Peace," the General yelled. With his right hand he grasped the Thing, as he had seen Ka do, and brought it down, hard, with anger, with hatred, on the head of the Professor.

Ka's skull split at the impact, and a stream of blood issued from his mouth. Without a moan, he slumped to the ground, reddening the rock around him.

The General, awed, stared at the device he held in his hand. Then he smiled, and it was a smile of triumph, cruel, merciless.

"Who's next?" he said.

The circle of motionless men, crouched around the great tree, fell silent, thinking. Baa, the bard, wiped away the sweat that had poured from his naked body during the exertion of his narration. Then he turned to the tree under which the Chief was seated and eating a thick root with evident relish.

"O mighty Szdaa," he said humbly, "I trust my story was to your liking."

Szdaa made a gesture of boredom. "I don't understand you young people. Or maybe I'm just getting old. You have a great imagination, my boy, no two ways about that. But I don't like science fiction . . . I prefer historical novels." He signaled to an old man with parchmentlike skin to come to him. "Good old Kgru," the Chief said. "You may not be a master of the New Song, but you still know how to tell stories that have some flavor. Your turn."

"Yes, mighty Szdaa," said Kgru. "I will now tell you a story of love, passion, and death. It's a tale that dates back to the last century and is called The Primate's Secret *or* The Mystery of the Missing Link.

1961

Industry and
Sexual Repression
in a Po Valley Society

The following study takes as its field of investigation
the urban agglomerate of Milan at the northern end
of the Italian peninsula, a protectorate of the Mediterranean Group. Milan is located at latitudes about
45° north of the Melanesian Archipelago and 35°
south of the Nansen Archipelago in the Arctic Glacial
Sea. Therefore it is more or less centrally situated as
far as the civilized world is concerned; but even
though it is fairly easily reached by the Inuit, it still
remains outside the purview of established ethno-
graphic research. I must thank Professor Korao Pal-
iau of the Anthropological Institute of the Admiralty
Islands for first suggesting I study Milan. Also, I was
able to pursue my fieldwork thanks to a generosity
of the Aborigine Foundation of Tasmania, which
awarded me a travel grant of twenty-four thousand
dog's teeth, enough to underwrite my expenses and
the purchase of required equipment. Nor could I
have written up my observations with the necessary
tranquillity had Mr. and Mrs. Pokanaou of Manus

Island not placed at my disposal a stilt house well away from the usual noise of the trepang fishermen and the copra merchants, who unfortunately have made certain areas of our once-peaceful archipelago uninhabitable. Nor could I have read my proofs and collated my bibliographical notes without the affectionate assistance of my wife, Aloa, always willing to interrupt her work of making *pua* garlands to rush to meet the mail boat, and bring to the stilt house the enormous cases of documents I regularly requested from the Anthropological Documentation Center of Samoa. Those cases would have been far beyond my strength.

For years investigators of the daily life and traditional customs of Western peoples have been guided by a priori theory, which effectively prevented the possibility of any real understanding. Dismissing Western peoples as primitive only because they practice machine worship and are still far from any direct contact with nature is a prime example of the false assumptions our ancestors made about peoples of no color, particularly Europeans. Holding to the erroneous historicist belief that in all civilizations analogous cultural cycles occur, the scientists thought, in examining the behavior of an Anglo-Saxon community, for example, that they were dealing simply with an earlier phase and that in the community's later development an inhabitant of, say, Glasgow would behave much like a Melanesian. We are therefore deeply indebted to the enlightened studies of Professor Poa Kilipak, who essayed the concept of "cultural model" and drew her brilliant conclusions. An inhabitant of Paris lives by a code of norms and habits that are part of an organic whole and constitute a given culture as valid as our own though very different. This new perception opened the way for an objective anthropological study of colorless man and an understanding of Western civilization. For—and I may be accused of cynical relativism—we are indeed dealing with a civilization, even if it does not conform to the ways of our own civilization. (Gathering coconuts by climbing a palm tree with bare feet is not necessarily a form of behavior superior to that of the primitive who travels by jet aircraft and eats fried potatoes from a plastic bag.)

The methods of the new anthropology, however, can also give rise to serious misinterpretations, especially when the researcher, precisely because he recognizes as an authentic culture the "model" he has investigated, bases his work on historical documents produced directly by its natives, attempting to derive from these the characteristics of that society.

1. The Hypothesis of Dr. Dobu of Dobu (Dobu)

A typical example of this "historiographic illusion" is furnished us, in fact, by the village of Milan, in a book published in 1910 by Dr. Dobu of Dobu (Dobu) entitled *Italian Villages and the "Risorgimento" Cult*. In this volume the well-known scholar attempts to reconstruct the history of the peninsula from documents written by the natives.

In the view of Dr. Dobu, the peninsula in the

course of the last century was the scene of fierce fighting aimed at bringing all the various villages under a single ruler. Some communities fought for this goal, while others opposed unification with equal ferocity. Dr. Dobu calls the former communities revolutionary or "risogimental" (a local dialect term referring perhaps to a rebirth cult, widespread in this period, surely shamanic), and the latter reactionary.

This is how Dr. Dobu, in his highly individual style, distinguished more by its ornate literary quality than by any scientific precision, describes the situation:

A risorgimental flame burned throughout the peninsula, but the reactionaries lay in wait, determined to keep patriots and the entire citizenry crushed beneath the heel of the Austrian. To be sure, not all the Italian states yearned for unification; but, first among them all, the kingdom of Naples was the one that held aloft the torch of freedom. According to the documents it was, in fact, the King of the Two Sicilies who founded the military academy of the Nunziatella, in whose halls were educated the fervent patriots Morelli, Silvati, Pisacane, and De Sanctis. This enlightened monarch was thus the prime mover of Italian rebirth; but in the shadows an obscure conspirator was weaving his sinister web: Mazzini, who is infrequently mentioned in the histories of the time, and then only in descriptions of the false plots he organized, always, curiously, discovered and foiled in time, so that the best and bravest patriots, cynically instigated by Mazzini, fell into the hands of the Austrian oppressor and were either imprisoned or executed. Another great enemy of risorgimento was Silvio Pellico. Even the most casual reader of Pellico's diary, written during his confinement in an Austrian prison, has the distinct impression that this book cost Italian unification more than one battle. The sly narrator paints an idyllic picture of a Moravian prison, a place of chaste repose where great human questions are debated with amiable jailers, where prisoners flirt, however platonically, with young ladies, and insects become pets. The prisoner welcomes an amputation, so impressed is he by the supreme skill of the Austrian surgeons, a skill which the amputees reward with floral offerings. And in his little work Pellico gives a subtle, cunning, and most dispiriting image of the Italian patriot, making him seem so alien to violence and combat, and, in the end, so impervious to any passion, so timid and sanctimonious, that the reading of these pages must surely have dissuaded legions of vigorous youths from fighting for national rebirth (just as in the lands of North America a little book entitled *Uncle Tom's Cabin* cast such discredit on the black slaves, making them seem foolish, ingenuous, and without initiative, that even today its influence is perceptible among the colorless in the southern states, who are irrevocably opposed to so inferior a race).

The Kingdom of Sardinia found itself in a singular position, apparently uninterested in the problems of national unification. It is known that the Piedmontese army intervened in Milan during a local insurrection, but succeeded in confusing the situation to such a degree that they caused the revolt to fail and abandoned the city and the rebels to the occupying Austrian forces. The prime minister, Cavour, was more concerned with serving the interests of other countries; first he helped the French against the Russians in a war to whose aims Piedmont was absolutely indifferent, then he went to great pains to provide foreign monarchs with the sexual favors of Piedmontese noblewomen. It is not evident that any other real effort was made to unify Italy beyond that of the Kingdom of the Two Sicilies. According to some texts, it was their inflexible devotion to rebirth that drove Piedmont to unleash against them an adventurer from Uruguay.

All these machinations had finally a single purpose: to clip the wings of the Italian power that, even more than the Two Sicilies, had been working ceaselessly toward unity not so much on the military level as through persuasion and philosophy. I refer to the Papal States. Exploiting the work of men of faith and intellect, the Papal States acted tirelessly to bring Italy together under a single government. It was a hard, impassioned struggle, in the course of which the Papacy had recourse even to subterfuge, luring, for example, crack Piedmontese troops to Rome to acquire a strong army for itself. This long and relentless struggle was concluded definitively only after a hundred years, on 18 April 1948, when finally the entire peninsula flocked to vote for the Papal party, whose Sign was the Cross.

Now, when the researcher approaches today's Milan, what does he see of the barbarian but politically complex situation that Dr. Dobu's ridiculous historiography would have us imagine? Alas, what the researcher sees leaves him a choice between only two hypotheses: one, that in the last fifty years some regressive phenomenon has taken place whereby every vestige of the political structure described by Dobu has disappeared; or two, that the community of Milan has not participated in the great developments that involved the rest of the Italian peninsula, because of the inhabitants' peculiarly colonial and congenitally passive nature, which is resistant to any acculturation and doomed to a frenetic social mobility quite common, for that matter, among primitive communities.

2. *La Pensée Sauvage*
(A Report on Field Research)

The typical day of the Milanese native obeys elementary solar rhythms. At an early hour he wakes and sets off to perform the tasks characteristic of this people: the gathering of steel in the plantations, the cultivation of metallic parts, the tanning of plastic materials, the barter of chemical fertilizers with the inhabitants of the interior, the sowing of transistors, the putting of motor scooters out to graze, the breeding of alfaromeos, and so on. The native, however, does not like his work and will do everything possible to postpone the moment when he has to start. Curiously, the village chiefs seem to assist him in this, eliminating, for example, the customary methods of transportation, digging up the tracks of the primitive tramways, confusing traffic with broad yellow stripes painted along mule tracks (with an obvious taboo power), and making deep holes in the least convenient places, where many natives are engulfed, probably sacrificed to local deities. It is hard to explain psychologically the attitude of the village chiefs, but this ritual destruction of transportation is no doubt linked with rebirth rites (obviously forcing hordes of inhabitants into the bowels of the earth, this human sacrifice considered seed to produce stronger, more vigorous individuals). But the population's reaction to this is a clearly neurotic syndrome, the attitude of the chiefs affording a genuine example of collective frenzy: "the tube cult." At regular periods the Rumor spreads through the community, and the natives are possessed by the quasi-mystic faith that one day enormous vehicles will move beneath the earth carrying individuals at miraculous speed to any part of the village. Dr. Muapach, a serious and learned member of my team, asked himself if the Rumor had originated with some real event, and then he descended into those caverns, but found nothing that could remotely justify this supposition.

A morning ritual shows how important the chiefs believe it is to keep the populace in a state of uncertainty. Every morning the members of the tribe read a hieratic message that the village headmen have distributed among the populace shortly after dawn, though the sheet bears the bewildering name of Il Corriere della sera, which in local dialect means courier of the evening. The hieratic nature of the message is underlined by the fact that what is communicated is totally abstract and has no relation to reality, though sometimes there is, as we have been able to verify, an apparent relevance, so that the native is given a kind of counter-reality or ideal reality in which he thinks he lives, as in a forest of living print: a world, in short, that is eminently symbolic and heraldic.

Kept always in this state of bewilderment, the native suffers a constant tension, which the headmen allow him to release only during collective feasts, when the whole population crams into immense constructions, ellipsoid in shape, from which an uninterrupted and frightful din is heard.

We tried, without success, to gain admission to one of these constructions; but with primitive yet shrewd diplomacy, the natives kept us out, demanding that we produce certain symbolic messages, which we learned were on sale. The sum we were asked, however, was such an exorbitant number of dog's teeth that, had we paid, we would have then had to curtail our research. Forced in this way to follow the ceremony from outside, we formed, on the basis of the loud and hysterical cries, a first hypothesis: that orgiastic rites were in progress. But as time went on, the horrible truth became clear. In these enclosures the natives devote themselves, with the chiefs' assent, to cannibalism, devouring human beings acquired from other tribes. The news of such gastronomic purchases is in fact circulated in the usual morning messages, where one can read daily a chronicle of them. From this chronicle it emerges that foreigners of darker skin colors are most highly prized, but also those from certain Nordic tribes and, in greatest quantity, Hispano-Americans. From what we could piece together, the victims are devoured in enormous collective courses according to complicated formulas publicly heralded in the streets, in which there are recommended recipes not unlike certain alchemistic numbers: "3 to 2," for example, or "4 to 0," or "2 to 1." Cannibalism, however, is not merely a religious practice but a widespread vice to which the whole population is addicted, as is demonstrated by the huge sums the natives seem prepared to spend on the purchase of human flesh.

Nevertheless, in some more affluent groups these Sunday banquets apparently inspire genuine horror, so that while the larger part of the population heads for the collective refectories, the dissidents flee desperately along all the roads leading out of the village, jostling one another in disorder, crushing one another with their vehicles, losing their lives in bloody brawls. As if, in the grip of a kind of maenadism, they viewed the path to the sea as their only escape, because the word most repeated during this sanguinary exodus is the local term for boat.

The low intellectual level of the natives is demonstrated by the fact that they are clearly unaware that Milan is not on the sea; and their mnemonic capacity is so scant that every Sunday morning they endure the same precipitous flight only to reenter the city that same evening in alarmed throngs, seeking refuge in their hovels, ready to forget, the following day, their blind adventure.

For that matter, virtually from birth, the young native is so trained that bewilderment and uncertainty inform his every act. In this respect the "rites of passage" are indicative. These take place underground, in chambers where the young are initiated into a sexual life characterized by an inhibitive taboo. Their tribal dancing is particularly instructive in this context. The young man and young woman stand face-to-face, shaking their hips, stepping first forward then backward, their arms bent at right angles, and they take care that their bodies never touch at any point. In these dances both participants demonstrate a total lack of interest in each other, and they move in reciprocal detachment. In fact, when one of the dancers bends to assume the usual position of the sexual act and imitates its rhythmic phases, the other draws back in apparent fear, bending at times, to elude the partner, all the way to the ground. When one dancer finally reaches the other and union can take place, the partner suddenly moves away, reestablishing the distance. The clear absence of sexual content in the dance (an authentic initiatory rite based on ideals of total abstinence) is complicated, however, by certain obscene details. Rather than display normally his naked member and swing it in a circle while the onlookers cheer (as one of our youths would do, in a ritual on the island of Manus or elsewhere), the male dancer keeps his scrupulously covered (I leave to the reader's imagination how repulsive this practice is even to the most sophisticated observer). Similarly, the female dancer never allows her breasts to be glimpsed, by their concealment thus stimulating desires that can only produce the profoundest frustration.

But frustration is an ideological component of the educational relationship which seems to operate in the assemblies of the elders, held in another confined space, where a kind of return to elementary natural-moral values is celebrated: a female dancer appears, lewdly covered with garments, and gradually removes them, exposing her limbs, so that the observer is led to believe that a cathartic resolution is in progress. Ideally it should conclude when the dancer is suitably naked. In reality—under precise orders of the headmen, as we have discovered—she retains certain fundamental garments at the end, or else pretends to remove them as she disappears in that same moment into the sudden darkness that fills the cavern. Thus the natives emerge from these places still in the grip of their lust.

But the basic question for the researcher is this: Are bewilderment and frustration truly programmed intentionally, by decision, or are these states also in part created by something deeper, which influenced that decision of the chiefs and priests, something which lies in the very nature of the Milanese habitat? A vexing question, because in the latter case we confront the profound wellspring of magic mentality that dominates the natives, we come up against the obscure Mothers who are at the origin of the dark night of the soul in this primitive horde.

3. The Paradox of Porta Ludovica
(An Essay on a Topological Phenomenon)

To explain the bewilderment, passivity, and resistance to enculturation also characteristic of these natives, other scientists have espoused the hypothesis originally proposed at the ethnological level by Professor Poa Kilipak. She formulated it in these terms: the Milanese native is in a condition of bewilderment because he lives in a "magic space" where the directions front, back, left, and right are not valid and consequently all orientation is impossible. There can therefore be no endeavor with a defined goal—hence the atrophy of various cerebral functions in the native, and a by-now-ancestral state of passivity. According to the native's understanding (or, actually, according to the scientists who favor positive acknowledgment of magic categories), the space where Milan stands is unstable, preventing any directional calculation and placing the individual in the center of coordinates that vary continually. It is therefore a *topological* space, like that of a microbe that chooses as its dwelling place a wad of chewing gum for the period of time (a "historical period" for the microbe, a geological era) in which the gum is chewed by a being of macroscopic dimensions.

"Milanese space" is excellently described by Professor Moa in his *Paradox of Porta Ludovica (A Study of Ambiguous Triangulation)*. All individuals, whether civilized inhabitants of the Marquis Islands or European savages, Moa asserts, move in space according to "orientative programs" carried out through triangulations. These triangulations are based on the assumption of a Euclidean plane geometry, taking as parametric models the forms of the square, the triangle, or the circle. For example, a savage of New York, accustomed to reaching the Hotel Plaza along a straight line from Washington Square, following Fifth Avenue to a point X, knows that by proper triangulation he can reach the same point via "a detour in the form of a square." In other words, he can follow the sides of the square West Eighth Street – Avenue of the Americas – Central Park South (a ninety-degree angle) – Grand Army Plaza – point X (the main entrance to the Plaza Hotel).

Similarly, a native of Paris who has followed the route Etoile – Place de la Bastille knows that he has touched two points of a circumference, covering one chord of it, but he could also reach l'Etoile from Place de la Bastille by following the circumference itself in the arc Bvd. Richard Lenoir – Place de la République – Boulevards Saint Martin – Saint Dénis – Bonne Nouvelle – de la Poissonière-Montmartre – Haussmann and finally Avenue Friedland to the Etoile.

The Porta Ludovica paradox is another matter altogether. Here is Profesor Moa on the subject:

> We will posit a Milanese native who has achieved an
> intelligence level capable of grasping abstractions.
> He formulates the simplest hypothesis concerning
> his habitat: namely, that Milan has a circular, spiral
> structure. Of course, no Milanese native could attain
> such a level of operative intelligence, precisely be-
> cause the topological space in which he lives prevents

him from conceiving any stable pattern. Rather, our hypothetical Milanese (as we have posited him) imagines Milan more or less as the surface of a painting by Jackson Pollock. Assume then that the subject in the past has had the following experience (also assuming that, having had the experience, he can remember it and extrapolate a pattern from it): he has learned that he can reach Porta Ludovica from Piazza Duomo along the straight line Via Mazzini – Corso Italia. Then he has learned that he can reach Piazza General Cantore (Porta Genova) from Piazza Duomo along the straight line Via Torino – Carrobbio – Via Correnti – Corso di Porta Genova. Concluding that the two straight lines represent radii of a circumference of which Piazza Duomo is the hub, he ventures to take the Piazza Generale Cantore – Porta Ludovica connection along the Viale D'Annunzio – Porta Ticinese – Via Giangaleazzo arc of the circumference. His attempt is crowned with success. So he then, unwisely, draws a general rule, as if the space in which he moves were stable and unchangeable, and ventures a further operation: having discovered the line Piazza Duomo – Via Torino – Via Correnti – Via San Vincenzo – Via Solari – Piazza Napoli, he interprets this as another radius of the same circle and thinks to connect Porta Napoli with Porta Ludovica by an arc of that circumference. He knows that the third radius is longer than the first two, and he knows therefore that the circumference where Piazza Napoli is located is beyond the circumference that includes Porta Ludovica. He decides therefore to alter his route at a certain point on this new arc, turning toward the center. He starts along the circumference arc by Via Troya, Viale Cassala, Viale Liguria, Via Tibaldi, Viale Toscana, Via Isonzo (slight turn toward the center), Viale Umbria, Viale Piceno, Via dei Mille, and Viale Abruzzi. Arriving at Piazzale Loreto, he turns again toward the center (otherwise, he knows, he will end up in Monza) and follows Viale Brianza, Viale Lunigiana, Viale Marche, and Via Jenner, turns again toward the center, adjusting his route, along Via Caracciolo, Piazza Firenze, Viale Teodorico, and Piazzale Lotto. At this point, afraid of still not having reached the inner coils of the spiral, he turns again toward the center, along Via Migliara, Via Murillo, Via Ranzoni, Via Bezzi, and Via Misurata. At which point he finds himself back in Piazza Napoli, having completed the circuit of Milan. Experiments show that after this the subject loses all capacity for telling direction. No matter how much he adjusts his course toward the center, reducing the apparent arc of the circumference, he will find himself at Porta Ticinese, Piazza Medaglia d'Oro, but never at Porta Ludovica. This leads to the supposition that Porta Ludovica does not exist for anyone in Milanese space who triangulates from Piazza Napoli. In fact, an attempt from any direction will inevitably be frustrated. All efforts at orientation must be made, if possible, independently of any preliminary notion of Milanese space. Actually, it will be impossible for the subject to refrain from falling back on spontaneous Euclidean references such as "If I take three steps to the left, then three steps forward, then three steps to the right, I will consequently be three steps ahead on the straight line that originates at my point of departure." As a rule, the subject, after a calculation of this sort, finds himself almost invariably in the Monforte district, which can be shown to be the geometric nexus of every possible destination. Milanese space stretches and contracts like a rubber band, and its contractions are influenced by the movements the subject makes in it, so that it is impossible for him to take them into account as he proceeds.

As all scientists know, Moa later attempted to demonstrate the Second Paradox of Porta Ludovica, making the hypothesis that with Porta Ludovica as the point of departure it would be impossible to identify the Monforte district (thus proving an exception to the postulate of the Monforte district as the geometric nexus of all possible destinations). But it is not known if his research proved successful, because Moa disappeared and his body was never found. There is a legend current among the natives that his restless spirit has roamed these many years around Piazza Napoli; having arrived there, it has never been able to leave. If this is what really happened, Moa has the distinction of having demonstrated the irreversibility of the Porta Ludovica paradox. A more alarming possibility, however, is that Moa's spirit haunts Piazza Napoli in a vain search for its body, which lies unburied in Piazza Tricolore, in the Monforte district.

Naturally philosophers found Moa's topological hypothesis unsatisfactory, and they have since tried to put the spatial ambiguity of Milan on a specific existential footing.

Still, Moa's topographical studies were the inspiration for the *Mailandanalyse* of Karl Opomat, a specialist in the Admiralty Islands trained in this sort of research during the period when those territories admitted, for acculturation workshops, a number of German "colonials."

> The being-in-Milan condition—Opomat writes—is equivalent to a being-around-Porta-Ludovica in the fictive world of the satisfiable. The in-what being-in-Milan comprises is, primarily, a system of reference; it is the that-which-to-what of the preliminary state, in allowing Porta Ludovica to approach. The in-what of self-referring comprehension was that-which-to-what of allowing Porta Ludovica to approach in the way of being proper to satisfiability; it is the phenomenon of being-in-Milan. But in the very Milanity of Milan in general *(Mailandischkeit von Mailand überhaupt)*, being-in-Milan must be clarified as Worry *(Sorge)*, and worrying-about, a worrying-about Porta Ludovica according to the three ecstasies of temporality, though in such a way that being-around-Porta-Ludovica can only be a being-around-Monforte.

Opomat's tragic view was to be tempered in later studies (cf. the notion of Piazza Napoli as "disrevelation"), but even these are not completely free of negativism.

Closer to the temporal situation illuminated by

Moa, on the other hand, is the penetrating phenomenology of another thinker, the late lamented Manoi Cholai, in whose unpublished manuscripts we find a dazzling analysis of the state of bewilderment in one who is inserted into the "fluxation" of the spatial Milanese situation.

Its [Milan's] present state of being is still in the originating source and diffusion *(Urquellen* and *Verquellen),* and in such a way that the diffusion is tantamount to a constant modification, which the actual present *(Urpräsent),* no-longer-originating present, transforms into a has-just-been, to which, however, a new originating present (Monforte district) is constantly added, which is both source and expansion, and to which a new mode is added of the now originating source, and so on. In Milan there is a phenomenon of reciprocal distancing *(Auseinandersein),* which is also a succession *(Nacheinander),* in the sense of a distancing of the points in time. In the movement from Porta Ludovica to Piazza Napoli both the now and the various has-beens *(Gewesenheiten)* are present at once, as well as the horizon of the maintaining *(Behalten)* and of the oncoming *(des Zukommendes).* Here we encounter, first of all, the medianness of intentional implication, with regard to retentive modification. From the source-point (Porta Ludovica) a later awareness of the just-has-been is diffused for the immediate has-been, which is enforced by a phase of awareness of the just-now or every just-now, and so we have a recursive of of of of. The retentive temporal flux is characterized in itself by a constant already-has-past, in which the already-past, in its individual stages, is characterized as the already-past of a passing and as an average or median passing, etc.

It is clear that the complexity of these analyses, impressive as they are, does not carry us very far beyond what Moa previously established, the fact that the mental backwardness of the Milanese native is due to the disorienting action of the ambiguity of the spatial situation on the nerve centers (directly influencing the inner ear, according to some representatives of traditional biological positivism, who tend, moreover, to speak not only of Eustachian tubes but also Fallopian, in the indigenous women who roam at night along the paths of the inner spirals of the city).

Nevertheless, we venture to refute both the philosophical explanation and the scientific-mathematical one, returning, instead, to a historical view which still incorporates the concrete anthropological research we have conducted (see Appendix, pp. 671–1346).

The primitive structure of the rites of passage and acts of worship, the colonial passivity, the static community, and the incapacity to evolve cannot be explained only by hairsplitting disquisitions on the spatial structure of the locality; they must be seen also in the light of profound economic and social factors.

Now, in comparing the present situation of the peninsula with that described in the historical writings of the natives which date back about a thousand years, we consider it appropriate to venture, at least as a historiographical hypothesis, the following explanation, believing that it is the most probable.

4. Church and Industry
(A Proposed Historical-socio-economic Interpretation)

The Italian peninsula is witnessing today what the natives would call a "struggle for turf." The social and political scene is dominated by two equally strong powers, disputing the control of the peninsula's territories and its people: Industry and the Church. The Church, according to statements recorded in the field, is a secular and worldly power, intent on earthly rule, on acquiring more and more property, on controlling the sources of political authority; whereas Industry is a spiritual power, bent on winning souls, on propagating mysticism and askesis.

During our stay on the Italian peninsula we observed some typical manifestations of the Church: the "processions" or "precessions" (obviously connected with equinoctial rites), which are unabashed displays of pomp and military force—including platoons of guards, police lines, generals of the army, and colonels of the air force. On another occasion, in the so-called Paschal celebrations, we witnessed outright military parades, in which whole armored units came to offer the symbolic homage that the Church demands of the army. This secular display of armed, uniformed power is totally different from the spectacle offered by Industry.

Its faithful live in gloomy conventlike buildings, where mechanical devices contribute to making the habitat more and more stark and inhuman. Even when such coenobia are constructed according to the dictates of order and symmetry, they are marked by a kind of Cistercian severity, for the coenobites' families live in small monastic cells in complexes that often cover amazingly vast areas. The spirit of penance pervades the congregation, especially the leaders, who, though wealthy, live in almost total poverty (I was able personally to confirm the extent of their incomes, declared publicly for penitential purposes). The leaders gather frequently in long, ascetic retreats called "board meetings," during which they sit for many hours, in gray habits, their faces haggard, hollow-eyed from fasting, to debate disembodied problems connected with the mystical purpose of the association: the "production" of objects as a kind of ongoing reenactment of divine creation.

These men seem to despise every symbol of wealth, and if they happen to have some gem or valuable fur, they rid themselves of it at once, donating it to the young maidens who act as vestals in the vestibules adjoining their hieratic sanctums. (These maidens gravely perform a sacred act similar to the spinning of prayer wheels by Tibetan monks, for they constantly tap the keys of an instrument that endlessly produces cryptic invocations to the divinity and exhortations to "productive" askesis.) The mystique of production also has a rigorous theological foundation. We were able to reconstruct a doctrine of the "circulation of merits," whereby the virtuous act of one member of the priestly caste can be used spiritually by another. In certain temples you witness the continuous passage of these "merits," or "bonds," during frenzies of religious ecstasy, when swarms of priests hasten to part with their "merits," diminishing their own value to make a gift of it to others, in an impressive crescendo of tension and hysterical *raptus*.

To the researcher it is clear that in the village of Milan the power that has gained ascendancy is Industry. As a result, the populace lives in a constant state of mystic excitement, which adds to the above-mentioned bewilderment, and produces a submissiveness to the decisions of the priests. The hypothesis of a magic space may therefore be not a metaphysical datum but, rather, a device of the religious powers designed to keep the Milanese faithful in a condition of detachment from all worldly values. And so the rites of passage take on new meaning, as do the pedagogy of frustration, the Sunday cannibalism, and the shamanic flight to the sea (which sacred drama seems a collective pretense, in which each player is at once conscious and helpless, convinced at heart that the solution lies not in flight but in total, loving surrender to the mystical power of production). Yet it would be erroneous to think of Industry as a power that governs the natives and the territory undisturbed. The Italian peninsula, scene of many and various events (of which Dobu gives an unfortunately mythological reading), represents a territory constantly open to invasion by barbarian peoples, to the immigration of hordes from the south who pour into the village and devastate it, changing its physical structure, camping at its outskirts, occupying the public buildings and arresting all administrative activity. In the face of this pressure from foreign hordes and of the corrupting action of the Church in its efforts to distract the natives' minds by tempting them with dreams of ill-conceived modernity (whose symbol can be found in the ritual game of Ping-Pong and in the electoral race, a debilitating blood sport in which even half-paralyzed old women take part), Industry stands as the last bulwark in the preservation of the old primitive civilization. It is not the role of the anthropologist to judge whether or not such preservation is a positive thing; he must simply record the function of Industry, which has erected for its goal white monasteries in which dozens upon dozens of monks, shut up in their cells and refectories (the *studia* or *officia studiorum*), sheltered from invasion, ruin, and uproar, and in the calm, inhuman neatness of their refuge, draft perfect constitutions for communities to come. These are silent, shy men, who appear only occasionally in the arena of public activity, to preach obscure and prophetic crusades, accusing those who live in the world of being "lackeys of neocapitalism" (an obscure expression, characteristic of their mystical speech). But once these addresses have been delivered, they again withdraw piously into their coenobia, recording their hopes on faded palimpsests. Protected by the spiritual power that governs them and the village, they are, to the scientist, the only key to understanding this disturbing and savage mystery.

1962

The End Is at Hand

"Heraclitus deposited the book in the temple of Artemis, and some say that he deliberately wrote it in obscure language so only those capable of reading it would approach it, and not in a lighter tone, which would expose him to the contempt of the crowd." Heraclitus himself said: "Why do you want to drag me here and there, you illiterates? I did not write for you, but for those who can understand me. One man to me is worth a hundred thousand; and the mob, nothing."[1]

But Heraclitus is gone, and his book has been thrown open to all the savant monkeys who desire to approach it, writing reviews and footnotes. And his disciples know more than he ever did. Which means that Heraclitus has been defeated by the mob, and, much to our sorrow, we witness today the triumph of mass-man. If your spirit has not yet withered completely, you have only to cross the

---

[1] Diogenes Laertius, *Lives of the Philosophers*, ix, 1–17.

agora on any ordinary day, and if you do not first choke with anguish (but is anyone left who can feel this precious emotion?) or succumb to social mimesis and join the euphorions who surround the latest philosophizer strolling in the public square, you will see those who were once the men of Greece: now perfect, smug automata crowing together amid the smells and cries, mingling with the Attic peasant who drives his flocks, the tuna merchants from Pontus Euxinus, the fishermen from Piraeus, the *emporoi* and the bawling crowd of *kapeloi,* the vendors of sausages, wool, fruit, pork, birds, cheese, sweets, spices, purgatives, incense and myrrh, plumes, figs, garlic, fowl, books, sacred fillets, needles, and coal—as our writers of comedy sometimes take pleasure in listing them. And in their midst you will see public inspectors circulating, money changers, controllers of weights and measures, copyists of poems, vendors of wreaths, all gathered in front of the humble shops, the tailors' stands; and you will see the makers of lutes and perfumes, the peddlers of sponges and whelks, the slave traders, and, crying their wares near the *hermai,* the women selling trinkets, bread, peas, and the cobblers, and the pimps.

Thus you can draw for yourself the portrait of mass-man, the citizen of democratic Athens, smug in his own cheap tastes, his Philistine fondness for conversation, his satisfaction with the philosophic alibi that the Lyceum and the Peripatos kindly offer him and with the noise in which he encloses himself like snail, the "distraction" which he has raised to the level of a religion. See the crowd as it clusters around the cockroach shape of the brand-new chariot acquired by Alcibiades, or as it rushes, sweating and vociferating, toward the latest messenger arriving from anywhere. Because the chief characteristic of mass-man is the desire to know, the lust for information. In contrast to the restraint of Heraclitus, who knew that wisdom was too precious a treasure to be placed at everyone's disposal, nowadays a certain Aristotle declares that "all men naturally desire knowledge," and the proof of this, he says, is "the pleasure they experience in sensations, which they love for themselves, independently of any profit, especially visual sensations."[2]

And what need be added to the negative anthropology of mass-man after this description of this indiscriminate desire to perceive, this greed for knowing, to see clearly and pleasantly and also from afar (a teleview, in short), a need apparently confirmed by his use of both metopes and pediments, where true proportions are altered and statues carved in such a way that they seem natural only to those looking at them from below. The sculptors thus cater to mass-man's laziness, and the prepackaged view thus relieves him of any obligation to interpret the obvious.[3]

In vain did our Montàlides recently decry this greed for information, whereby it seems almost that the disk of our earth is enclosed in a "sphere of psychism, its density in constant expansion," given

[2] *Metaphysics*, 1980a.
[3] See also Plato's nonchalant remarks in *The Sophist*, 235–236.

that "an ever-thicker blanket of information and of views projected from a distance covers the world we inhabit."[4] This pervasive illiteracy no longer makes any impression on Athenian mass-man; nor could it, since from his school days his educators' only concern was to "inform," with no hesitation about corrupting him by the pages of contemporary poets, as we were indeed warned (but with smug, vainglorious hypocrisy) by that crony Plato, still admired by the conformist crowd, when he said that "our teachers do as they are desired to do. And when the youth has learned his letters and begins to understand what is written . . . he finds on the desk in front of him, to be read and to be memorized perforce, the works of great poets . . . so that the youth, imitating them, will desire to become like them."[5] What is to be done? The culture industry is too content with its achievements to listen to the voice of wisdom (but isn't that out of fashion in any case?), and so we will have to witness the development of students who, when they are thirty, will go around at night to decapitate the *hermai,* as a young intellectual of our acquaintance has done. From such teachers we cannot expect better disciples. The production of mass-man is coming to fruition.

But, then, did we not theorize his need to be and stay with others, rejecting the joys of silent solitude? Such is the essence of so-called democracy, whose first commandment seems to be: Do as others do and

---

[4] Cf. "Λα φωνδουτα ψιχικα," Κωρριερη δηλλα Σηρα, 24 III 63.
[5] *Protagoras* XV (Modern Library ed., p. 213).

obey the law of the greatest number. Anyone is worthy of holding any office, provided he collects enough people to elect him. For the less important posts trust in luck, as mass-man's logic is by nature aleatory. "Cities must truly be made up of elements that are equal, as far as possible, and homogeneous: a condition found especially in the middle class . . . Thus Phocylides properly expresses this wish: 'The best condition is the mean, and that is the place I want to occupy in the city.'[6] Such is the view of Aristotle, to whom, *vox clamantis in deserto*, Ortegaygassetos replied in vain, denouncing the fact that "since the second half of the last century there has been in Europe a noticeable exteriorization of life . . . Private existence, hidden and solitary, closed to the public, to the crowd, to others, becomes increasingly difficult . . . The street has become stentorian."[7] We would say, the agora has become stentorian, but the agora is mass-man's ideology, it is what he has always wanted and what he deserves. It is only right that Plato should stroll there and converse with his adherents: that is his realm, and mass-man cannot live alone, for he must know everything that is happening and must speak about it everywhere.

And nowadays he *can* know everything. You see what happened at Thermopylae. Only a day after the event a messenger brought the news, and someone had already thought to package it, simplifying and

---

[6] *Politics*, IV, 9, 1295b.
[7] "Σοχιαλιθαθιονε δελλ θομω," Λο Σπεττατορη.

reducing it to an advertising slogan: "Our arrows will hide the sun. Good! We will fight in the shade!" The echolalic Herodotus had done his duty to that tyrant, the crowd with a hundred ears.

And thus the so-called historians, who are nothing but eager reporters of the present, seem to be exactly where they belong. Efficient chief PR man for Pericles, Herodotus can find nothing better to write about than the Persian wars. (A pure and simple news report, in other words. We could hardly hope, these days, for a Homer, one who possesses the poetic lucidity required to write about things he has neither seen nor heard, endowing them with the dimension of fable.) Herodotus only has to read three or four Ionic logographs and he can claim to know everything. He talks about everything. And, as if that were not enough, he then begat an even more pompous and arid Thucydides, who, after the shameful debacle of the fall of Amphipolis (which he failed to prevent, a failure both of arms and of administration), forgot his Peloponnesian misadventures and created a new persona as a chronicler, agreeing to describe the events of the war *as they were occurring*. Had we thus finally scoured the lowest depths of gutter journalism? No, because after him came Xenophon, master of an art capable of making even a laundry list a historical document; Xenophon, who whimpers over a commonplace eye ailment. (Characteristic of the cultural industry is its vulgarity, the insistence on the coarse but striking detail. Is a river crossed? Then the crosser will be "wet to the navel."

Do the men eat rotten food? They will "flow from behind.")[8] But in Thucydides there is more than this; we find in him the desire, common, to write literature, to become a candidate for the literary prizes the culture industry provides for those able to follow the fashion. Thucydides does not hesitate to dot his prose with naturalistic decorations, imitating the nouveau roman: "The surface of the body did not reveal excessive warmth to the touch, nor pallor to the sight; it was reddish, livid, covered with little sores and ulcers . . ."[9] Subject? The plague in Athens.

Thus, having reduced the human dimension to the objective styleme, up-to-date reporting and the avant-garde dominate our new literature. For anyone with a glimmer of intelligence the only reply to the distress of Bobtoweridas, who complains that the language of the younger writers is incomprehensible, must be: There is nothing to comprehend, nor does mass-man wish it otherwise. The eclipse of Attic man is now total.

But if there is a decline of the West, mass-man does not let it bother him. Does he not live in the best of all possible worlds? Read again the speech of Pericles to a content and enthusiastic Athenian crowd: We live in a meritocratic society, where the dialectic of *status* is exalted with blithe optimism ("If a man is useful to the city, neither poverty nor an obscure social position will be any hindrance to him"), and

---

[8] *Anabasis*, passim.
[9] *Peloponnesian War*, II, 48–54.

so the criterion of discrimination, whereby the *aristos* was precisely that, the best, is submerged in the leveling frenzy. Attic man is now happy to live as a face in the crowd, a white-chlamys worker, slave to conformist behavior ("We have an incredible fear of falling into illegality: we are obedient to those who follow one another in the government, obsequious to the laws, particularly those laws that arouse the universal scorn of those who fail to follow them"). Attic man now lives happily as the representative of a leisure class ("To refresh us after our toil we have found many diversions for our spirit, celebrating according to ancient custom games and feasts that continue throughout the year, while we live in houses supplied with every comfort, where daily pleasure dispels all sadness"). In other words, Attic man is the inhabitant of a prosperous state, an affluent so-ciety ("Goods of every kind flow into our city, and so we can enjoy not only all the fruits and products of this country, but with equal pleasure and ease those of other countries, as if they were ours").[10]

Can we stir this mass-man, content in his Attic village, from his mindless, smug sloth? No, for he is held there by those very games that Pericles men-tions. Consider the crowds that flock to Olympia and argue about the last *meta* as if their very souls were at stake; or that the Olympic Games now serve for numbering the years! Life seems to be measured by the feats of a victor in the throwing of the javelin, or by him who runs a certain course ten times. The

---

[10] *Peloponnesian War*, II, 37–41.

outcome of the pentathlon is the gauge of *arete*. Some will commission a poet to compose an anthem for such "heroes," and the crown they receive enhances the glory of the city. Pericles's oratory has truly given us the idea of a civilization in which *everything is beautiful*. Provided you have renounced your own humanity. As Montàlides warned, "the universal human community will be an aggregate of cellular aggregates, a bank of madrepores in which each individual will be inserted and catalogued not according to his mind but according to his productive possibilities or his greater or lesser integration into the pattern of total leveling."[11] We look back at the Pharaoh's solitude and isolation as a lost paradise, but Attic man feels no nostalgia for it, because he has never tasted its flavor: on the ramparts of Olympia he celebrates his melancholy apocalypse unawares. Decision is not expected of him, in any case. The culture industry has provided him now with the virtually electronic contortions of Pythia of Delphi, who in epileptic spasms gives him advice about future action. All in sentence fragments deliberately incomprehensible, language regressed to the irrational, for the consumption of the awed and democratic crowds.

In the past, culture could be asked to offer a word of salvation; today salvation has been reduced to a game of words. Attic man is possessed by an appetite for public debate, as if it were necessary to discuss every problem and obtain general agreement. But

---

[11] "Μαδρεπορε ουμανη," Κωρριερη δηλλα Σηρα, 14 IV 1963.

sophistry has debased truth to public consensus, and public debate seems the ultimate refuge for this mass of talkers.

We can only underline the bitter reflections of Bloomides, which cleverly reproduce the conversation that preceded the unseemly rush to debate. "Hey, would you come to the agora tomorrow for a round-table discussion of truth?" "No, but why not ask Gorgias? He'd be ideal for a eulogy of Helen, too. And you might try Protagoras, his theory of man as the measure of all things is the latest fashion, you know?" But Bloomides' appeal against debate remains unheard, and the polemicist labors in vain to refute the pernicious ideology that lies behind the impassioned wranglings before a lazy, corrupted public.

Instead, the culture industry will offer Attic mass-man, if debate does not satisfy him, a wisdom even more immediate, diluted, moreover, in attractive digests, as his taste demands. And the master of that art is the abovementioned Plato, who has a real gift for presenting the harshest truths of ancient philosophy in the most digestible form: dialogue. Plato doesn't hesitate to turn concepts into pleasant and superficial examples (the white horse and the black horse, the shadows in the cave, and so on), bowing to the demands of mass-culture. So what was deep (and what Heraclitus was careful not to bring into the light) is raised to the surface, up to the level of comprehension of the most idle listener. The final infamy: Plato does not hesitate to use the sublime problem of the One and the Many as a subject for the conversation of men who withdraw into the shop of a smith (none of them able to think except in "noise"!), while he takes care to make the debate appetizing through the clever use of suspense and the game of nine hypotheses, which have all the captivating charm of quiz programs with cash prizes. *Eristics and Maieutics* (these are the names given by the reporters, happy to conceal their emptiness by employing the latest terms) still have the familiar function: Attic man need make no effort to understand; the experts of the culture industry will give him the illusion that his mind is achieving a comprehension that is in fact ready-made. The game begins with the magic tricks (skillful, we must admit) of that old satyr Socrates, who even managed to transform his well-deserved death sentence into a monstrous advertising campaign. Socrates remained to the end a faithful servant of the culture industry, providing the pharmaceutical firms with that slogan: "Hemlock is good for you." Or: "What's all this about corrupting kids? I don't know what you're talking about. After a hard day in the agora, what I need is a nice glass of hemlock!"

End of the farce: a cock to Aesculapius, the final hypocrisy. We have to agree with the learned Zollaphontes when he says, "The more the mass-media offer spectacles that are removed from humanity, from true dialogue, the more they assume a false tone of private conversation, of jovial cordiality, as we can see (if our spirit can bear it) by beholding their productions, which obey a secret rule: Interest man in what has no interest for him, aesthetic, economic, or moral." [12] What better definition for the Socratic-Platonic potpourri of the *Symposium*, where under the pretext of a philosophical dialogue we witness the spectacle of convivial incontinence, coarsened by clear, indecent sexual allusions. Similarly, in the *Phaedrus* we read that when a man *looks* (for the final phase is, inevitably, a civilization of *voyeurs*) at his beloved, "sweat bathes him, and an unusual heat invades him; thus descending in him, through the eyes, a flow of beauty, and a new warmth spreads . . . Everything swells, everything grows, from its roots upward, and the growth extends under the whole soul . . . and the wing begins to swell." [13] Thinly disguised obscenity: this is the final gift, mass-erotica peddled as philosophy. As for the relations between Socrates and Alcibiades, that is biography; and the culture industry exempts them from aesthetic criticism.

Still too "natural" to become an industry, sex has, in any case, become commerce, as Aspasia tells us. Commerce and politics: sex is integrated into the system. Phryne's gesture reminds us sadly that even faith in uncorruptible judges is ill founded. To these contradictions and catastrophes of the human spirit the culture industry has a ready answer: such scandals are of use, they supply the raw material for the authors of tragedies. This process confirms the final apocalyptic abyss of Attic man, the path of his irreparable degeneration.

---

[12] Εχλισσε δηλλ ιντελλεττυαλε, p. 60.
[13] *Phaedrus*, 23–30.

You see the Athenians, still in broad daylight, take their places in the long tiers of seats in the amphitheater, where with stupid, dazed expressions they will become caught up in events enacted by some poor mummers stripped of all humanity, since the mummers have concealed their faces behind the grotesque fiction of masks, and their elevated shoes and padded costumes mimic a greatness not their own. Like ghosts that display no nuance of feeling, no shifts of passion, exposed to the shameless attention of all, they offer you debate on the most awful mysteries of the human spirit: hatred, parricide, incest. Things that in the past people would have concealed from the eyes of the crowd now become the source of general entertainment. And here again the public must be entertained according to the dictates of mass-culture, which obliges you not to allow an emotion to be intuited but, rather, to present it ready-made to the consumer. Thus it will not be a poetic expression of lament but a stereotyped formula of grief that suddenly assaults you with studied violence: "Alas, alas, alas! Ototòi totòi!" But what else can be expected of authors who hire out their art and know they must slap together a product that the archon will accept or reject as he chooses? It is common knowledge that sponsorships these days go to prolific citizens, and therefore the culture industry could not find more straightforward legislation. You offer the backer what he asks of you, and what he asks of you will be evaluated by weight and quantity. You know very well that if you want to see a play of yours staged, you can't submit it singly. No, you must offer a whole tetralogy complete with satyr-drama. Hence there is creation on demand, poetry machine-made, by formula. And the poet, if he is to see his work performed, must also be composer and choreographer and dance master, forcing the chorus shamefully to kick their legs to the immodest whine of the flute. The ancient author of the dithyramb is now transformed into the producer of an Attic Broadway; and the askesis he has finally achieved is that of the pimp.

Shall we analyze the course of this regression? It began with Aeschylus, who, naturally, is adored by mass-man. Aeschylus made poetry out of the latest headlines: take the battle of Salamis. Fine stuff for poetry! A military-industrial achievement whose technological details the author lists with a delight that no longer shocks our jaded sensibilities. The "oars striking loudly in unison to the cadence," the vessels with their "bronze prows," the "beaks" of the "massed ships pressed in a strait," the ships with their "bronze cheeks" that, clashing, "snapped all the aligned oars," the maneuvers that the Greek ships made around the Persians, "girding them"—all this with a heavy, arrogant taste for mechanical detail, a passion for including in the numbered verses snatches of everyday conversation, nomenclature worthy of some instruction manual, and in a secondhand style that, if we had any sense of discrimination left, would make us blush.[14] As Zollaphontes puts it, "The character of the industrial mass is perfectly caught here:

---

[14] *Persians*, cf. 386–432.

it vacillates between hysteria and gloom. Sentiment has no place among the worshipers of Baal."[15] Sentiment? And when he has to describe a scene of majesty and death, what does he fall back on? The vocabulary, the slang of a butcher. "And they still, like tuna caught in a net, with stubs of oars, with broken carcasses, slammed down, crushed backs, to moans and howls, and on all sides the expanse of sea was smoking . . ."[16] In its desperate attempt to *refaire Doeblin sur nature,* the culture industry foists on us a language that has been made into a mere thing, an artisan's tool, a mechanism, a shipyard's terminology.

But do not think that with Aeschylus we reached the nadir. The scandal goes deeper. With Sophocles we have finally the perfect example of enforced somnambulism mass-produced for the crowd. While Sophocles has renounced Aeschylus's religious neuroses, and distanced himself also from the elegant *boulevardier* skepticism of Euripides, the practice of *sophrosyne* in his work becomes the alchemy of moral compromise. He turns out all-purpose situations, and thus has no true purpose. Take Antigone. Here you have the whole shebang. The girl devoted to her brother, barbarously slain. The wicked and insensitive tyrant. The principles sacrosanct even at the price of death. Haemon, son of the tyrant, a suicide because of the girl's sad fate. Haemon's mother, following him to the grave. Creon aghast at all the deaths

---

[15] Εχλισσε, p. 25.
[16] *Persians,* 386ff.

caused by his insane Philistinism. Soap opera, thanks
to the Attic culture industry, has reached its climax,
its abyss. And as if that wasn't enough, Sophocles
seals his work with moral commentary. In the first
stasimon we have the glorification of technological
productivity: "Many are the wondrous things in the
world, but none is more wonderful than man . . .
He wears out the Earth, supreme divinity, year after
year following his young horses, driving his plow
and turning the soil . . . Tribes of wild beasts, of
marine creatures, he snares in his woven nets . . ."[17]
So we have the ethic of productivity, praise for the
stupid work of the mechanic, the allusion to prole-
tarian genius. "We must be pleased," Zollaphontes
observes ironically, speaking of the relationship between literature and industry, "with the victory of
the genius who now slays monsters with technology,
and we must hope that that victory is put to good
use for man."[18] Such is the ideology of mass culture.
And Sophocles, a master of this, does not hesitate to
add to protagonist and deuteragonist . . . we have a
triagonist, too, and decoration of the scene,[19] since,
obviously, to impose ready-made emotions the classic stage was not enough for him. Before long we
shall see the introduction of a fourth interlocutor,
one completely dumb, and then tragedy will have
taken the final step, which is the comedy of superfetation, achieving total incommunicability in servile

---

[17] *Antigone*, I, first stasimon.
[18] Ἐχλισσε, p. 19.
[19] Cf. Aristotle, *Poetics*, IV, 15.

obedience to the rules of the avant-garde theater, *en attendant* its Godòtes.

And now, for Euripides, the time is ripe. He is just innocent and radical enough to win the favor of the masses, able to reduce drama to *pochades,* as can be seen from the insistent *plaisanteries* of Admetus and Hercules, which neutralize what's left of the power of tragedy in *Alcestis.* As for *Medea,* here mass culture performs its star turn, entertaining us with the private neuroses of a bloodthirsty hysteric and a plethora of Freudian analysis, offering a perfect example of how to be the Tennessee Williams *des pauvres.* You're given the full dose: how is it possible not to weep and to feel terror and pity?

Because this is what tragedy requires. You must feel terror and pity, and feel them on command, on cue. Just read what Aristotle, that peerless master of hidden persuasion, has to say on the subject. Here is the whole recipe: Take one protagonist endowed with such qualities that the public both admires him and deplores him; make terrible and pathetic things happen to him, sprinkling the mixture with an appropriate amount of sudden reversals, agnitions, catastrophes; stir well, bring to a boil, and *voilà,* you have cooked up what is called catharsis, and you will see the audience tear its hair and groan with fear and sympathy, crying out for relief. You shudder at these details? It's all written down; read the texts of this Choryphée of contemporary civilization. The culture industry is quick to circulate them, convinced that if not falsehood then sheer spiritual laziness will further its aims.

Ideology? If there is one: Accept what is given and use it as a tool of persuasive argumentation. The most recent, infamous handbook by this Aristotle, *Rhetoric,* is nothing less than a catechism of marketing, a motivational inquiry into what appeals and what doesn't, what's believed and what's rejected. Now you know the irrational stimuli that govern the actions of your fellows, he says, and therefore your fellows are at your mercy. Push their buttons: they are yours. With this work, as Zollaphontes observes, "we have a fabrication that does not reflect the natural tendencies of the public but calculates its effects as far as salability goes, heightening the colors according to the laws of brute reaction to stimuli."[20] The effect? *Delectatio morosa* or, in other words, foreplay, the forge of every vice. Fantasy, daydream. Tragedy gives this the highly visible seal of social approval, raising a temple to a monster appearing from the shadows of a barbaric society.

But I don't want to give the impression that the poor Boeotian victim is being defrauded only in the state amphitheater, on the day of the performance. Aristotle himself, in his *Politics* (Book 8), talks about music and "its sensible effect on our temperament." Study the rules of songs as imitations of the stirrings of the soul, and you will learn how to "stir the emotions," you will see that the Phrygian mode leads to orgiastic behavior, the Doric mode to "virility." Need anything be added? Here you have a textbook for the emotional manipulation of the *korai* or, as

---

[20] Εχλισσε, p. 42.

they say nowadays, *teenagers.* Enforced somnambulism is no longer a utopian dream, it is a reality.
These days the flute is played everywhere, though
the great Adornòs inveighed at length against it.
Thanks to Aristotle's popularizing, musical skill is
within everyone's grasp, and it is taught to children
in school. In no time a song of Tyrtaeus will become
an air anybody can whistle in the baths or on the
banks of the Ilissus. Music and tragedy now show
us their true face: a manipulation of the emotions,
which the crowd rushes blissfully to accept, welcom-
ing this role of masochism.

It is from the lecterns of hidden persuaders that
our young people are educated, transformed into a
flock of sheep in the gymnasia. When they are adults,
the same science of public opinion will teach them
how to behave in communal life, reducing virtue,
sentiment, and true talent to a mask. Hear what
Hippocrates has to say: "For the doctor it is obviously an excellent testimonial to appear well fed
and healthy; the public will believe that he who
cannot take proper care of his own body will not be
able to attend to the bodies of others . . . A doctor
entering the room of a patient must be careful how
he sits, how he acts; he must be well dressed, with
serenity in his expression . . ."[21] Falsehood becomes
a mask; the mask becomes the person. One day, in
the not-too-distant future, to define man's most profound being the only term left will be mask, *persona,*
which denotes the most superficial appearance.

---

[21] *Corpus Hippocraticum,* passim.

Enamored of his own appearance, mass-man will be able to enjoy only what *appears* real, he will take pleasure only in *imitation*,[22] that is to say the parody of what is not. You see this in the lust found in painting (where the highest praise is reserved for illustrators whose painted grapes birds would swarm to peck at) and in sculpture, supremely skilled now in reproducing naked bodies that seem real, or lizards scuttling tree trunks who lack only the power of speech, as the vulgar exclaim ecstatically. And in red figure vases they have begun to introduce forms seen frontally, as if the traditional profile did not suffice to suggest, through poetic allusion, the full object of the imaginative gaze.

But artistic production now bears the heavy yoke of industrial necessity, and crafty mass-man has slyly transformed that necessity into choice. Art bows to the laws of science: among the columns of temples you now see golden proportions established, which the architect hails with the enthusiasm of a surveyor; and Polycletus supplies you with a "canon" for the production of perfect, industrialized statuary, for his *Doryphoros*, as has been noted bitterly, is no longer a work but a poetics, a treatise in stone, a concrete example of a mechanical rule.[23] Art and industry now move in step; the cycle is achieved; the spirit cedes its place to the assembly line; cybernetic sculpture is perhaps already at the gate. The last stage of initiation

---

[22] *Poetics*, IV, 55.
[23] Cf. Galen, *De placitis Hippocratis et Platonis* V. Cf. also Pliny, *Nat. Hist.* XXXIV.

is the herd solution. Ephebes are lined up in regimenting exercises. Healthy revolt against the father is replaced by surrender to the group, against which the youth is incapable of defending himself. Egalitarianism undermines every difference between old and young, and the episode of Socrates and Alcibiades confirms this. With such leveling, the expression of personal feelings atrophies. Thus today's model of Attic man will remain unchanged until death and beyond. The manufacturing of emotion, having pervaded everyday life, will be imposed also on the last breath. Not you but professional mourning women will mime a sorrow of which you are now incapable; as for the deceased, the great step will not suffice to make him give up the little sordid pleasures to which he clung in life. In his mouth you will place a coin (the pretext is an obol for Charon) and a cake for Cerberus. For the rich you will add toiletries, weapons, necklaces.

And this same undiscriminating mass will form the audience that flocks to enjoy the cheap pornography of Aristophanes. The mysterious connection between Love and Hate, which the pre-Socratic philosophers barely led us to suspect, already bores them. As for knowledge, all has now been reduced to a temporary learning; it is enough to memorize the theorem of Pythagoras (every Boeotian knows this dreary little trick with triangles), while Euclid has agreed to melt down all mathematical wisdom into a conventional and undemonstrable postulate. Before long, the schools doing their part, everyone will know how to read and do sums and will demand nothing further, except perhaps that the right to vote be extended to women and resident aliens. Is it worth resisting? Who can summon the strength to oppose the mounting tide of vulgarity?

Soon everyone will want to know everything. Euripides has already tried to make the Eleusinian mysteries common knowledge. For that matter, why retain any area of mystery now, when the democratic constitution gives everyone the leisure to idle away his time at the abacus and the alpha and beta? Reporters tell us that a certain Mesopotamian artisan has invented a thing called a water wheel, which turns on its own power and moves a grindstone thanks simply to the flow of a river. Thus the slave formerly in charge of the mill will have time to devote to the stylus and the waxed tablet. But as a gardener from some distant Eastern country said when confronted with a similar device: "I once heard my master say: He who uses the machine becomes the machine. He who is a machine in his work has the heart of a machine . . . I do not know your invention, but I would be ashamed to use it." Citing this pithy apologue, Zollaphontes asks: "How can a worker ever aspire to holiness?"[24] But mass-man does not aspire to holiness; his symbol is the great beast depicted for us by Xenophon, the slave of his own thirst, who writhes on the ground like a crazed monkey, shouting: "Thálatta, thálatta." Will we perhaps forget that nature "makes the bodies of free men different from those of slaves" and that "men

---

[24] Εχλισσε, p. 113.

are slaves or free by right of nature," as Aristotle, in one of his more lucid moments, asserted?[25] Will we yet manage to elude, even a handful of us, the occupations that mass culture assigns to a race of slaves, attempting to involve also the free man? Then the free man's only recourse is to retire, if he has the strength, into his private contempt, his private grief. Unless one day the culture industry teaches even the slaves their letters, and undermines that last foundation of the aristocracy of the spirit.

1963

---

[25] *Politics*, I, passim.

Letter to My Son

Dear Stefano,

Christmas is marching upon us, and soon the big stores downtown will be packed with excited fathers acting out their annual scenario of hypocritical generosity, having joyfully awaited this moment when they can buy for themselves—pretending it's for their sons—their cherished electric trains, the puppet theater, the target with bow and arrows, and the family Ping-Pong set. But I will still be an observer, because this year my turn hasn't yet come, you are too little, and Montessori-approved infant toys don't give me any great pleasure, probably because I don't enjoy sticking them in my mouth, even if the manufacturer's label assures me that they cannot be swallowed whole. No, I must wait, two years, or three or four. Then it will be my turn; the phase of mother-dominated education will pass, the rule of the teddy bear will decline and fall, and the moment will come when with the sweet and sacrosanct violence of pa-

ternal authority I can begin to mold your civic con-
science. And then, Stefano . . .

Then your presents will be guns. Double-barreled
shotguns. Repeaters. Submachine guns. Cannons.
Bazookas. Sabers. Armies of lead soldiers in full
battle dress. Castles with drawbridges. Fortresses to
besiege. Casemates, powder magazines, destroyers,
jets. Machine guns, daggers, revolvers. Colts and
Winchesters. Chassepots, 91's, Garands, shells,
arquebuses, culverins, slingshots, crossbows, lead balls,
catapults, firebrands, grenades, ballistas, swords, pikes,
battering rams, halberds, and grappling hooks. And
pieces of eight, just like Captain Flint's (in memory
of Long John Silver and Ben Gun), and dirks, the
kind that Don Barrejo so liked, and Toledo blades
to knock aside three pistols at once and fell the
Marquis of Montelimar, or using the Neapolitan feint
with which the Baron de Sigognac slayed the evil
ruffian who tried to steal his Isabelle. And there will
be battle-axes, partisans, misericords, krises, javelins,
scimitars, darts, and sword-sticks like the one John
Carradine held when he was electrocuted on the third
rail, and if nobody remembers that, it's their tough
luck. And pirate cutlasses to make Carmaux and Van
Stiller blanch, and damascened pistols like none Sir
James Brook ever saw (otherwise he wouldn't have
given up in the face of the sardonic, umpteenth
cigarette of the Portuguese); and stilettos with tri-
angular blades, like the one with which Sir William's
disciple, as the day was gently dying at Clignancourt,
killed the assassin Zampa, who killed his own mother,
the old and sordid Fipart; and pères d'angoisse, like

those inserted into the mouth of the jailer La Ramée while the Duke of Beaufort, the hairs of his coppery beard made even more fascinating thanks to the constant attention of a leaden comb, rode off, anticipating with joy the wrath of Mazarin; and muzzles loaded with nails, to be fired by men whose teeth are red with betel stains; and guns with mother-of-pearl stocks, to be grasped on Arab chargers with glistening coats; and lightning-fast bows, to turn the sheriff of Nottingham green with envy; and scalping knives, such as Minnehaha might have had, or (as you are bilingual) Winnetou. A small, flat pistol to tuck into a waistcoat under a frock coat, for the feats of a gentleman thief, or a ponderous Luger weighing down a pocket or filling an armpit à la Michael Shayne. And shotguns worthy of Jesse James and Wild Bill Hickok, or Sambigliong, muzzle-loading. In other words, weapons. Many weapons. These, my boy, will be the highlight of all your Christmases.

Sir, I am amazed—some will say—you, a member of a committee for nuclear disarmament and a supporter of the peace movement; you who join in marches on the capital and cultivate an Aldermaston mystique on occasion.

Do I contradict myself? Well, I contradict myself (as Walt Whitman put it).

One morning, when I had promised a present to a friend's son, I went into a department store in Frankfurt and asked for a nice revolver. Everyone looked at me, shocked. We do not carry warlike toys, sir. Enough to make your blood run cold. Mortified, I left, and ran straight into two Bundes-

wehr men who were passing on the sidewalk. I was
brought back to reality. I wouldn't let anybody fool
me. From now on I would rely solely on personal
experience and to hell with pedagogues.

My childhood was chiefly if not exclusively bel-
licose. I used blowpipes improvised at the last minute
among the bushes; I crouched behind the few parked
cars, firing my repeater rifle; I led attacks with fixed
bayonets. I was absorbed in extremely bloody bat-
tles. At home it was toy soldiers. Whole armies
engaged in nerve-racking strategies, operations that
went on for weeks, long campaigns in which I mo-
bilized even the remains of my plush teddy bear and
my sister's dolls. I organized bands of soldiers of
fortune and made my few but faithful followers call
me "the terror of Piazza Genova" (now Piazza Mat-
teotti). I dissolved a group of Black Lions to merge
with another, stronger outfit, then, once in it, I
uttered a pronunciamento that proved disastrous.
Resettled in the Monferrato area, I was recruited
forcibly in the Band of the Road and was subjected
to an initiation ceremony that consisted of a hundred
kicks in the behind and a three-hour imprisonment
in a chicken coop. We fought against the Band of
Nizza Creek, who were filthy dirty and awesome.
The first time, I took fright and ran off; the second
time, a stone hit my lips, and I still have a little knot
there I can feel with my tongue. (Then the real war
arrived. The partisans let us hold their Stens for two
seconds, and we saw some friends lying dead with a
hole in their brow. But by now we were becoming
adults, and we went along the banks of the Belbo

River to catch the eighteen-year-olds making love, unless, in the grip of adolescent mystical crises, we had renounced all pleasures of the flesh.)

This orgy of war games produced a man who managed to do eighteen months of military service without touching a gun, devoting his long hours in the barracks to the grave study of medieval philosophy. A man of many iniquities but one who has always been innocent of the squalid crime of loving weapons and believing in the holiness and efficacy of warrior values. A man who appreciates an army only when he sees soldiers slogging through the muck after the Vajont disaster, engaged in a peaceful and noble civic purpose. A man who absolutely does not believe in just wars, who believes wars are unjust and damned and you fight always with reluctance, dragged into the conflict, hoping it will end quickly, and risking everything because it is a matter of honor and you can't evade it. And I believe I owe my profound, systematic, cultivated, and documented horror of war to the healthy, innocent, platonically bloody releases granted me in childhood, just as when you leave a Western movie (after a furious brawl, the kind where the balcony of the saloon collapses, tables and big mirrors are broken, someone shoots at the piano player, and the plate-glass window shatters) cleaner, kinder, relaxed, ready to smile at the passerby who jostles you and to succor the sparrow fallen from its nest—as Aristotle was well aware, when he demanded of tragedy that it wave the blood-red flag before our eyes and purge us totally with the divine Epsom salts of catharsis.

Then I imagine the boyhood of Eichmann. Lying on his stomach, with that death's bookkeeper expression on his face as he studies the Meccano pieces and dutifully follows the instructions in the booklet; eager also to open the bright box of his new chemistry set; sadistic in laying out the tiny tools of The Little Carpenter, the plane the width of his hand and the twenty-centimeter saw, on a piece of plywood. Beware of boys who build miniature cranes! In their cold and distorted minds these little mathematicians are repressing the horrid complexes that will motivate their mature years. In every little monster who operates the switches of his toy railway lies a future director of death camps! Watch out, if they are fond of those matchbox cars that the cynical toy industry produces for them, perfect facsimiles, with a trunk that really opens and windows that can be rolled up and down—terrifying! A terrifying pastime for the future commanders of an electronic army who, lacking all passions, will coldly press the red button of an atomic war!

You can identify them already. The big real-estate speculators, the slumlords who enforce evictions in the dead of winter; they have revealed their personality in the infamous game of Monopoly, becoming accustomed to the idea of buying and selling property and dealing relentlessly in stock portfolios. The Père Grandets of today, who have acquired with their mother's milk the taste for acquisition and learned insider trading with bingo cards. The bureaucrats of death trained on Lego blocks, the zombies of bureaucracy whose spiritual decease began with the rubber stamps and scales of the Little Post Office.

And tomorrow? What will develop from a child-hood in which industrialized Christmases bring out American dolls that talk and sing and move, Japanese robots that jump and dance thanks to an inexhaustible battery, and radio-controlled automobiles whose mechanism will always be a mystery? . . .

Stefano, my boy, I will give you guns. Because a gun isn't a game. It is the inspiration for play. With it you will have to invent a situation, a series of relationships, a dialectic of events. You will have to shout boom, and you will discover that the game has only the value you give it, not what is built into it. As you imagine you are destroying enemies, you will be satisfying an ancestral impulse that boring civili-zation will never be able to extinguish, unless it turns you into a neurotic always taking Rorschach tests administered by the company psychologist. But you will find that destroying enemies is a convention of play, a game like so many others, and thus you will learn that it is outside reality, and as you play, you will be aware of the game's limits. You will work off anger and repressions, and then be ready to receive other messages, which contemplate neither death nor destruction. Indeed, it is important that death and destruction always appear to you as elements of fantasy, like Red Riding Hood's wolf, whom we all hated, to be sure, but without subsequently harbor-ing an irrational hatred for Alsatians.

But this may not be the whole story, and I will not make it the whole story. I will not allow you to fire your Colts only for nervous release, in ludic purgation of primordial instincts, postponing until later, after catharsis, the *pars construens*, the communication of values. I will try to give you ideas while you are still hiding behind the armchair, shooting.

First of all, I will teach you to shoot not at the Indians but at the arms dealers and liquor salesmen who are destroying the Indian reservations. I will teach you to shoot at the Southern slave owners, to shoot in support of Lincoln. To shoot not at the Congo cannibals but at the ivory traders, and in a weak moment I may even teach you to stew Dr. Livingstone, I presume, in a big pot. We will play Arabs against Lawrence, and if we play ancient Romans, we'll be on the side of the Gauls, who were Celts like us Piedmontese and a lot cleaner than that Julius Caesar whom you will soon have to learn to regard with suspicion, because it is wrong to deprive a democratic community of its freedom, leaving as a tip, posthumously, gardens where the citizens can stroll. We'll be on the side of Sitting Bull against that repulsive General Custer. And on the side of the Boxers, naturally. With Fantomas rather than with Juve, who is too much a slave of duty to refuse, when required, to club an Algerian. But now I am joking: I will teach you, of course, that Fantomas was a bad guy, but I won't tell you, not in complicity with the corrupt Baroness Orczy, that the Scarlet Pimpernel was a hero. He was a dirty Vendéen who caused trouble for the good guy Danton and the pure Robespierre, and if we play French Revolution, you'll participate in the taking of the Bastille.

These will be stupendous games. Imagine! And

we'll play them together. Ah, so you wanted to let us eat cake, eh? All right, M. Santerre, let the drums roll! Tricoteuses of the world, unite and let your knitting needles do their worst! Today we'll play the beheading of Marie Antoinette!

You call this perverse pedagogy? And you, sir, antifascist practically since birth, have you ever played partisans with your son? Have you ever crouched behind the bed, pretending to be in the Langhe valleys, crying, Watch out, the Fascist Black Brigades are coming on the right! It's a roundup, they're shooting, return the Nazis' fire! No, you give your son building blocks and have the maid take him to some racist movie that glorifies the extinction of native Americans.

And so, dear Stefano, I will give you guns. And I will teach you to play extremely complicated wars, where the truth will never be entirely on one side. You will release a lot of energy in your young years, and your ideas may be a bit confused, but slowly you will develop some convictions. Then, when you are grown up, you will believe that it was all a fairy tale: little Red Riding Hood, Cinderella, the guns, the cannons, single combat, the witch and the seven dwarfs, armies against armies. But if by chance, when you are grown up, the monstrous characters of your childish dreams persist, witches, trolls, armies, bombs, compulsory military service, perhaps, having gained a critical attitude toward fairy tales, you will learn to live and criticize reality.

1964

Three Eccentric Reviews

Bank of Italy, *Fifty Thousand Lire,*
Italian National Mint, Rome, 1967

Bank of Italy, *One Hundred Thousand
Lire,* Italian National Mint, Rome, 1967

The two works under examination could be described as *éditions numerotées* in folio. Printed on both recto and verso, they also reveal, against the light, a delicate watermarking, a product of the most skilled craftsmanship and a technology rarely achieved by other publishers (and then only with great effort and often at disastrous economic risk).

Still, while these works possess all the characteristics of a collector's edition, actually an immense number of copies has been printed. This publishing decision, however, has not resulted in an economic advantage to the collector, for the price is still beyond the reach of many fanciers' pocketbooks.

The paradox—editions that on the one hand flood

the market and on the other can be valued only (forgive the expression) by their weight in gold—causes also the eccentricity of their circulation. Perhaps inspired by the example of municipal libraries, the amateur, to have the pleasure of possessing and admiring these editions, must be prepared to make serious sacrifices, but he will then quickly pass the works on to another reader, so that the edition keeps circulating, going from hand to hand. Inevitably the copies deteriorate through use, yet this wear and tear does not diminish their value. It might even be said that wear and tear makes these works more precious, so that those who wish to possess them redouble their efforts and energy, prepared to pay more than the list price.

These facts underline the ambitious nature of this publication, which has met with the widest approval, though the venture must be justified by the intrinsic value of the product.

And indeed, when the critic starts examining the actual stylistic merit of the works under review, some doubts about their validity begin to surface, even the suspicion that the reading public's enthusiasm is due to a misconception or else inspired by speculative aims. First of all, the narrative is in many respects incoherent. For example, in *Fifty Thousand Lire* the watermark appears on the recto, symmetrically opposite the head-and-shoulders portrait of Leonardo da Vinci, and this image can be interpreted as Leonardo's Saint Anne or Virgin of the Rocks; but in *One Hundred Thousand Lire* it is hard to conceive what relation, if any, exists between the apparently

Hellenic woman in the watermark and the portrait of Alessandro Manzoni. Is the woman perhaps his Lucia interpreted in a neoclassical style, painted or engraved by an earlier artist like Appiani, who had somehow foreseen the creation of Manzoni's heroine? Or could she be—but here we sink to the most obvious and scholastic allegory—the image of an Italy that has some filial connection with the Lombard novelist? An exaggeration of the political activity of the author of *Carmagnola* or a typical avantgarde device reducing ideology to language (Manzoni father of the Italian language and hence father of the nation, etc., etc.—a dangerous syllogism in the style of Gruppo 63!). The narrative incoherence can only put the reader off, and in any case it will have a deleterious effect on the taste of the young, so we must hope that at least they and the less educated classes will be kept well away from these pages, in their own best interest.

But the incoherence goes deeper. In the context of such fastidiousness, whether neoclassical or bourgeois-realistic (the portraits of the two artists and the landscapes of the verso seem based on the canons of the cheapest sort of socialist realism: a concession to the policies of our center-left coalition?), it is hard to see any reason for the violent insertion of the exotic motive "Payable to the Bearer," which evokes the vision of an African safari and a line of blacks laden with bales of merchandise, forming a queue to obtain something in exchange for their extorted labor, a scene right out of Rider Haggard or Kipling and surely inappropriate to the subtext here.

But the incoherence found at the level of content appears also at the formal level. What is the purpose of the realistic tone of the portraits, when all the surrounding decoration is clearly inspired by psychedelic hallucinations, presented like the visual diary of a Henry Michaux journey into the realm of mescaline? With vortices, spirals, and undulant textures the work reveals its hallucinatory purpose, its determination to summon to the mind's eye a universe of fictive values, of perverse invention . . . The obsessive repetition of the mandala motif (every page includes at least four or five radiating symmetries of obvious Buddhist origin) betrays a metaphysics of the Void.

The work as pure sign of itself: this is the end result of contemporary literary theory, and these editions confirm it. Perhaps there are collectors who aspire to gather these pages in a volume, potentially infinite, as happened with Mallarmé's *Livre*. Vain effort, because the sign that refers to other signs is lost in its own vacuity, behind which, we suspect, no real value exists.

An extreme example of the cultural dissipation of our time. These works have been received by readers with an approbation that in our opinion bodes only ill: the taste for novelty conceals the aesthetic of obsolescence—of consumption, in other words. The numbered copy that we have before our eyes still seems to promise us, through the number that distinguishes it, the possibilities of possession *ad personam*. Which is a fraud, because we know that the current aesthetic taste for conspicuous consumption will soon

lead the reader to seek out more copies, other print-
ings, as if to find in constant exchange the guarantee
that the single copy cannot provide. A sign in a
world of signs, each of these works becomes a way
to distract us from things. Its realism is bogus, as its
psychedelic *avant-gardisme* only hides deeper alien-
ations. In any case, we are grateful to the publisher
for having sent us these free copies for review.

1967

L'Histoire d'O
(Draft of a Review
for *Ladies Home Journal*)

How much time, and how much trouble should a
woman take in preparing herself for an evening with
her fiancé? We have already dealt with this problem
several times in our column, but we are prompted to
address it again after the publication of this little
book, probably the work of a famous international
visagiste who has coyly chosen to hide behind the
pseudonym of Pauline Réage.

One reason the book can be recommended is the
attention it devotes to details of toilette often ne-
glected by how-to books and women's magazines,
even though such details are of supreme importance.
Our readers therefore can find helpful hints about
fixing iron rings around ankles and wrists, accessories
usually ignored since they require a great deal of care
to ensure they are fastened securely. It's a great
mistake to rely on the guarantee of some masked

blacksmith; for excellent devices can be found at any beauty salon, or else by telephoning SADE, the Society for Assistants in Deflowering and Emasculating, who will send a masseur to your home within minutes. You must make certain that the iron causes those unsightly red weals, the drops of blood and the chafed wrists and ankles that your Special Man is so crazy about. The ring should be secured just as our grannies used to buckle their chastity belts, not too loose and not too tight. Only a gentle little nip to create that allure of tense haughtiness along with the moist, frightened-gazelle look, and Mister Right is yours!

Even greater care (allow at least an hour before your date arrives) is a must when it comes to attaching a golden padlock to your labia majora. Madame Réage's book shows clearly how this operation can be performed in a few, easy steps. Unfortunately, she doesn't list retailers that carry the item in question, but if you rummage carefully through Mom's trunks up in the attic, you may make some amusing discoveries. A woman who knows how to love is bound to be clever in recycling odds and ends, putting them to new and thrilling uses.

And now a final reminder (the book is full of fantastic advice on this subject): Be imaginative and decorate your body with all sorts of long bloody gashes, using your little boudoir whip with the studded thongs. The best whips come from Barcelona, though lately the rival Hong Kong whips have been the rage (but beware of the imitations from East Germany). When you're making these marks, however, don't overdo it. The book explains clearly how your man can add more love marks, especially if he counts melancholy English gentlemen among his best friends. We're assuming he works for some multinational and is highly connected. Otherwise, Mme. Réage's advice is best forgotten, because her book is aimed, after all, at the upmarket reader. If you're not in that class (face facts!) you might try another first-rate booklet, *Official List of Infirmities and Mutilations Acceptable for Exemption from Military Service*. It's available to our readers from its publisher, the Ministry of Defense.

1968

D. H. Lawrence, *Lady Chatterley's Lover*

Finally a breath of fresh air. Your reviewer's overwhelming sensation is a chaste and modest emotion as he begins speaking of this book, which has just arrived on his desk like a comet at Bethlehem in the murky firmament of obsessive contemporary erotica. In a galaxy of Justines tortured by the latest Marquises d'O and of Emanuelles carrying out the most refined experiments in coitus interruptus, and of multiple couples who copulate and recopulate in geometric swappings, in an era of magazines for women only (but read obviously by men only) and sado-masochistic comic books, an era when a film can create a scandal only if a heterosexual woman, fully dressed, is happily married to her husband who works at the First National Bank (giving the well-to-do an uneasy hint of the irreparable decadence of their behavior), and as human sexuality becomes the object of excessively scrupulous examination in the pages of *Our Sunday Visitor* and sexual congress for the purpose of reproduction now arouses psychoses far beyond the worst descriptions of Krafft-Ebing—here, at last, is a clean, straightforward love story, absolutely unsophisticated, the sort of read our grandmothers used to enjoy.

The plot is simple: a noblewoman, brought up (and revolted) by the consumer values of our technological era, falls in love with a gamekeeper. Obviously the gamekeeper comes from a different background, an earthly paradise totally uncontaminated, with no notion of the pollution of the atmosphere (though he is not unaware of sexual pollution) or ecological mutation. Their love is pure, a series of marvelous experiences, free of the slightest hint of perversion, an encounter between the sexes strictly according to the laws of nature, as in those old-fashioned love stories now read only by the fanatics of nostalgia, determined to rediscover in the jumble of secondhand stalls those tales that the culture industry no longer dares reprint because of its ambivalent, cowardly conformism to anticonformity.

Here, then, is a book the younger generation should read. It would help them form a cleaner, more modest view of life, entertain genuine feelings, not adulterated, and develop a taste for simple, honest things, like the smell of new-mown hay or baking bread.

A book, too, for frustrated, restless wives, for

happy brides, and for wandering husbands seeking a basic redefinition of family life. A book for dissatisfied couples in search of truth. A book whose limpid, sober pages, free of all fetishistic gratification, point the way to a healthier relationship, rejuvenating it, supplying its vexed boredom with the fundamental values that any normal person wishes to see restored.

The narrative style is occasionally marred by decadent mannerisms, and we would advise the author to follow less blindly the debatable sophisms of Marshall McLuhan in conducting his analysis of contemporary society. Here and there some residual traces of class consciousness emerge, for example, the author's embarrassment in describing the relations between his leading characters. He would do well to work for more realism in his handling of the erotic scenes, which to our contemporary taste seem tied still to the apron strings of Victorian *pruderie*. He should tackle a theme of this sort more freely, boldly calling acts, situations, and parts of the body by their real names.

All the same, this is a book of great power, of great idealistic breadth, open, innocent, delicately romantic. Reviewers will unhesitatingly recommend it as required reading in the schools, as an antidote to the excesses of contemporary eroticism now assailing our tender and vulnerable young people. This book is a timely reminder that uncorrupted values such as Life, Nature, and Sex still exist and can be perceived in their virginal and virile reality.

1971

The Discovery of America

DAN: Good evening, folks. Here it's 7 P.M. on the 11th of October 1492, and we're linked directly with the flagship of the Columbus expedition, which by 7 A.M. tomorrow should put Europe's first thalatanaut on a new land, a new planet, if I may be allowed the metaphor, that Terra Incognita so many astronomers, geographers, cartographers, and travelers have dreamed of. Some claim that this land is the Indies, reached from the West rather than from the East; others say it's actually a whole new continent, enormous and unexplored. As of now, in a joint effort, all our TV networks will be transmitting around the clock, twenty-five hours. We're linked with the telecamera installed on the flagship, the *Santa Maria*, and with our relay station in the Canary Islands, as well as with Sforza TV in Milan, and the Universities of Salamanca and of Wittenberg.

Our guest here in the studio is Professor Leonardo da Vinci, the famous scientist and futurologist, who will provide a running commentary, explaining the technical details of this extraordinary venture. But first a word from Jim. Jim?

JIM: Well, Dan, as you know, unfortunately we won't be able to see the actual landing. Our camera's attached to the figurehead of the caravel, but the antenna, in the crow's nest of the mainmast, can't be activated until after the lookout has sighted landfall and the sails are furled. Where are the three caravels now, in their epoch-making voyage? I tell you, we're all holding our breath while we follow this adventure, the most daring exploit of all time. It's the beginning of a new age, which some columnists have already suggested calling The Modern Era. Man is emerging from the Middle Ages and is making a major break-through in his intellectual evolution. Obviously, the crew at Cape Canary feel the same way we do . . . But I'd like to hear from Alastair Cook, who has just arrived from London especially to take part in this historic broadcast. Alastair? Can you hear me?

ALASTAIR: Loud and clear, Jim. Can you hear me?

JIM: Alastair?

ALASTAIR: Yes? You hear me?

JIM: Go ahead, Alastair. We've got audio.

ALASTAIR: As I was saying. Yes, I hear you splendidly. It's a tense moment here at Cape Canary. The position of Christopher Columbus's three galleys—

JIM: Sorry to interrupt, Alastair. Actually, I don't believe the ships are galleys. They're—

ALASTAIR: Hang on, Jim . . . They're telling me . . . there's such a racket here in the control center. Three hundred scalzed Carmelites are simultaneously saying solemn High Masses for the success of the

voyage . . . Yes, mmm, yes . . . You're right, Jim.
They're not galleys. They're xebecs. A typical Mediterranean vessel used for—

JIM: Um, Alastair . . . over the audio I'm hearing
the word "caravels" . . .

ALASTAIR: How's that, Jim? I've lost you . . . You
can't believe the confusion here . . . What? Oh,
right. As I was saying, he has three caravels, the
Nina, the *Pan*—no, the *Pinta,* and the *Santa Rade-
gonda* . . .

JIM: Er, Alastair, the press kit says it's the *Santa
Maria.*

ALASTAIR: Right you are, Jim! One of the boys here
is saying the same thing. But there's a difference of
opinion about whether it's the Santa Maria . . . In
any case, a caravel is a typical Mediterranean vessel,
and our technical department has prepared a scale
model . . . By the way, this uniform I'm wearing is
from the Spanish navy. How do you like it? Now,
the caravel, as I was saying, is—

JIM: Sorry to interrupt you, Alastair, but Professor
Vinci's here in the studio with us, and he can perhaps
tell us something about the caravel from a propulsion
point of view . . .

LEONARDO: Deman retep taerg a . . .

JIM: Hang on a minute, control room. Professor
Vinci has a kind of, well, you might call it a quirk
. . . He talks from right to left, so you'll have to
reverse the ampex. If you recall, we arranged a nine-
second delay for this reason, between recording and
transmission. Ready with the ampex? Can you hear
me? Roll it!

LEONARDO: A great Peter named—

JIM: Excuse me, Professor Vinci . . . This is a family program, you understand . . . So if we could stick to the subject . . .

LEONARDO: Mmm, of course, I'm so sorry. Now then, the caravel exploits the propulsion system known as *ventus et vela*, that is, wind and sail, and it stays afloat in accord with the principle of Archimedes by which a body immersed in a liquid receives an upward impulse equal to the weight of the water displaced. The sail, the fundamental element in propulsion, is articulated in three sections, main, mid, and jib. The bowsprit has a special function, coordinating flying jib and staysail, whereas the topgallant and the spanker operate in an orientative sense.

JIM: Does the thalattocraft reach its destination whole, or are certain stages detached during its trajectory?

LEONARDO: I'm glad you asked that question, Jim. There's a process of stripping the thalattocraft usually known as "hit and drown." In other words, when a sailor behaves improperly toward the admiral, he receives a blow on the head and is thrown into the sea. This is the moment of the so-called mutiny showdown. In the case of the *Santa Maria* there have been three hit and drowns, which are exactly what has allowed Admiral Columbus to maintain control of the thalattocraft, with what might be called manual operation—using the hands, in other words. In such instances the admiral has to look sharp and act at precisely the right moment . . .

JIM: . . . otherwise he loses control of the craft, I understand. Tell me, Professor, what is the technical function of the cabin boy?

LEONARDO: Very important, Jim. It's known technically as the "feedback function." Perhaps our viewers would get a better idea if we called it the "release valve." I have devoted considerable study to this problem, and, if you like, I can show the viewers some of my anatomical drawings, which—

JIM: Thanks a lot, Professor, but I'm afraid we have to move right along. We have a linkup also with the Salamanca studio. Are you there, Willard?

WILLARD: You betcha, Jim. I'm here in Salamanca. Great place, Salamanca! And I've got some brainy guys for you to interview. Really swell people. First I'd like to ask a question of the President of the University of Salamanca. Just stay at that chalk line, Prexy, eh? Now tell us, Doctor, er, what exactly is this America everybody's talking about?

PRESIDENT: Nonsense, that's what it is! Horse feathers!

WILLARD: Hold on a sec, Prexy. Our experts have written a word . . . Con . . . Continent.

PRESIDENT: Well, I'm sorry for your experts. No, no . . . I supplied you people with a basic text, the Almagest of Ptolemy. Check and you'll see that the chances of discovering anything are practically nil. Admiral Columbus apparently thinks he can *buscar el levante por el ponente,* in other words, sail east to find the West, but his project is absolutely without any scientific foundation. Most people are quite aware that the Earth ends beyond the pillars of Hercules.

The survival of the three vessels after that boundary is due to a simple televisual effect, the work of the devil. The Columbus case is the obvious result of the weakness of the proper authorities in dealing with student protest, and on this subject I am preparing a book, in fact, for the Bob Jones University Press. But even if such a voyage were possible, the thalattocraft would inevitably lack sufficient cruising range, through a shortage of angelic fuel. You see, William, as various councils have taught us, the problem is knowing how many angels can stand on the head of a pin. In the council reports there is no mention of angels standing on the top of a foremast. That would instead be Saint Elmo's fire, and therefore diabolical manifestations unsuited to directing a caravel toward a promised land or terra incognita, however you choose to call it.

WILLARD: Yeah, well, this is heavy stuff, and I don't want to get into an argument here. We'll see what the experts have to say, and meanwhile good luck with the great work you're doing at the university! Now we'll hear from a very important expert, a lovely gent who is the Dean of the Royal Society of Cartographers of Portugal. Tell us, Mr. Dean, do you think Columbus is really heading for the Indies?

DEAN: That's a tough question, Willard, and Columbus's big mistake is that he's waiting to give an empirical answer instead of working out a definition of the problem through its essence. The fact is, you see, *non sunt multiplicanda entia sine necessitate*, which leads us to postulate the existence of one and only one India. In that case, Columbus should land from the east at the westernmost tip of Asiatic soil, to be precise, at the mouth of the river Ussuri. If this proves to be correct, then his expedition is of no interest whatsoever, given the total political and geographical unimportance of that land. Or he could reach the eastern end of the island of Gipango—I believe you call it "Japan"—in which case the Mediterranean economy will experience a severe negative counterreaction. Since the people of that island perversely specialize in producing transistorized imitations of the mechanical inventions of others, the market of the seafaring republics will be invaded by thousands of perfectly imitated caravels and at much lower prices. The economy of the republic of Venice will collapse, unless the Doge's authorities provide for the construction of new shipyards at Porto Marghera, but that would have disastrous consequences for the ecological balance of the lagoon and the islands . . .

WILLARD: Now we have another super-guest with us here, the Dean of the law school of the University of Granada. He's going to fill us in on the legal aspects of this discovery. A lot of people are wondering who'll be the owner of these new lands. And the part of the ocean Columbus has crossed, who will that belong to?

LAW DEAN: The questions of international law raised by this expedition are serious. First of all, there is the problem of a division between Spain and Portugal, and I think I am not rushing things when I suggest a summit meeting should be convened, say, at Tordesillas, to establish a theoretical line of demarcation between the spheres of influence . . .

ROBIN: Excuse me, Willard . . . This is TV Sforza in Milan. We have a group of distinguished Milanese judges here in the studio, and they don't agree. They say that the problem as stated doesn't make sense. That at that rate you would have to consider another important maritime power, England, and then it is even conceivable that one day the new lands would be divided into Anglo-Saxon, Spanish, and Portuguese spheres of influence . . . Pure science fiction, of course! Now I'll turn the line over to Wittenberg. All yours, Johnny!

JOHNNY: Here's . . . Wittenberg! Our guest is a young and very smart Augustinian student of theology here at Wittenberg U. He's considered the white hope of Holy Mother Church, and we have a question for him. Tell us, Dr. Luther, do you think this landing represents a genuine, lasting revolution in human history?

LUTHER: Let me put it this way: technological revolutions aren't the only kind. There are also inner reformations that can have much greater, more dramatic, thrilling results . . .

JOHNNY: Brilliant, Doctor . . . But surely you don't mean to say that in the future inner reformations will make even more of a wave than this great scientific event . . . ?

LUTHER: Believe, don't believe . . .

JOHNNY: Ha ha, that's what I'd call sibylline. Just joking, Doc. I'm ready to believe you. My motto is: Believe Firmly and Sin Strongly. Ha ha ha!

LUTHER: Clever phrase, that. I'll just make a note.

JIM: Excuse me, fellows. One moment. I'm getting voices over the audio . . . It seems land has been sighted . . . Yes, now I can hear them clearly. They're shouting, "Land ho!" Can you hear them, Alastair?

ALASTAIR: Actually, no. Half a mo', I'll check with the Azores.

JIM: Yes! Land has definitely been sighted . . . The ship's dropping anchor . . . They've landed!! Today, October 12, 1492, man has set foot for the first time in the New World. Alastair, what are they saying where you are?

ALASTAIR: Well . . . the latest is that it seems the landing has been postponed for a month, that the land sighted was the Aeolian Islands . . .

JIM: No, no, Alastair, I heard it distinctly!

DAN: Hello? Yes? Fine. Looks like both Jim and Alastair are right. The ship has definitely dropped anchor, as Jim says, but it still isn't terra firma. It's San Salvador. A little island in the Caribbean archipelago, which some geographer has also decided to call the Sea of Tranquillity. But now the camera set on the flagship's figurehead is operational. Now here's Christopher Columbus setting foot on the beach, to stick the flag of His Catholic Majesty in the sand! It's a great sight, folks. Among the palm trees a crowd of natives with feathers in their hair are coming out to meet our thalattonauts. We're now about to hear the first words uttered by man in the New World. They are being uttered by a sailor leading the group, the bosun, Baciccin Parodi . . .

PARODI: *Mamma mia*, Cap'n, look at them tits!

JIM: What did he say, Alastair?

ALASTAIR: I didn't hear very well, but it wasn't what we have in the press kit. One of the engineers says it must have been interference. This apparently happens a lot in the New World. Here we are! Admiral Columbus is about to speak!

COLUMBUS: A small step for a sailor, a giant step for His Catholic Majesty . . . Hey, what's that they're wearing around their necks? Holy shit, that's gold! Gold!

ALASTAIR: The spectacle the cameras are giving us is truly grand! The sailors are running toward the natives with great leaps, man's first leaps in the New World . . . From the necks of the natives they are collecting samples of the New World's minerals, cramming them into big plastic bags . . . Now the natives are also making great leaps, to get away. Apparently the lesser gravity would cause them to fly off, so the sailors are fastening them to the ground with heavy chains . . . Now the natives are all neatly lined up in a civilized way, while the sailors head for the ships with the heavy bags filled with the local mineral. The bags are extremely heavy, and the men have had to make a huge effort to fill them and carry them . . .

JIM: It's the white man's burden, Alastair!

1968

Make Your Own Movie

In 1993, with the final, complete adoption of video cameras even in the offices of the national registry, cinema both commercial and underground was in real trouble. The *prise de la parole* had by now tranformed moviemaking into a technique within everyone's reach, and everyone was watching his or her own film, deserting the movie theaters. New methods of reproduction and projection in cassettes insertable into the dashboard of the family car had made obsolete the primitive equipment of the avant-garde cinema. Numerous handbooks were published on the order of *Be Your Own Antonioni*. The buyer bought a "plot pattern," the skeleton of a story which he could then fill in from a wide selection of variants. With a single pattern and an accompanying package of variants an individual could make, for example, 15,741 Antonioni movies. Below we reprint the instructions that came with some of these cassettes. The letters refer to the interchangeable elements. For example, the basic Antonioni pattern ("An empty lot. She walks away") can generate "A maze of McDonald's with visibility limited due to the sun's glare. He toys for a long time with an object." Etc.

Antonioni Scenario

An[x] empty[y] lot.[z] She[k] walks away.[n]

Variants Key

x   Two, three, an infinity of. An enclosure of. A maze of.

y   Empty. As far as the eye can see. With visibility limited due to the sun's glare. Foggy. Blocked by wire-mesh fence. Radioactive. Distorted by wide-angle lens.

z   An island. City. Superhighway cloverleaf. McDonald's. Subway station. Oil field. Levittown. World Trade Center. Stockpile of pipes. Scaffolding. Car cemetery. Factory area on Sunday. Expo after closing. Space center on Labor Day. UCLA campus during student protest in Washington. JFK airport.

k   He. Both he and she.

n   Remains there. Toys for a long time with an object. Starts to leave, then stops, puzzled, comes back a couple of paces, then goes off again. Doesn't go away, but the camera dollies back. Looks at the camera without any expression as he touches her scarf.

Jean-Luc Godard Scenario

He arrives[a] and then bang[b] a refinery[c] explodes. The Americans[d] make love.[e] Cannibals[f] armed with bazookas[g] fire[h] on the railroad.[i] She falls[l] riddled with bullets[m] from a rifle.[n] At mad speed[o] to Vincennes[p] Cohn-Bendit[q] catches the train[r] and speaks.[s] Two men[t] kill her.[u] He reads sayings of Mao.[v] Montesquieu[z] throws a bomb[w] at Diderot.[x] He kills himself.[k] He peddles *Le Figaro*.[j] The redskins arrive.[y]

Variants Key

a   Is already there reading the sayings of Mao. Lies dead on the superhighway with brains spattered. Is killing himself. Harangues a crowd. Runs along the street. Jumps out of a window.

b   Splash. Splat. Wham. Rat-tat-tat. Mumble mumble.

c   A kindergarten. Notre Dame. Communist Party headquarters. Houses of Parliament. The Parthenon. The offices of *Le Figaro*. The Elysée. Paris.

d   The Germans. French paratroopers. Vietnamese. Arabs. Israelis. Police.

e   Do not make love.

f   Indians. Hordes of accountants. Dissident Communists. Crazed truck drivers.

g   Yagatan. Copies of *Le Figaro*. Pirate's sabers. Submachine guns. Cans of red paint. Cans of blue paint. Cans of yellow paint. Cans of orange paint. Cans of black paint. Picasso paintings. Little red books. Picture postcards.

h   Throw rocks. Bombs. Empty cans of red paint, green paint, blue paint, yellow paint, black paint. Pour some slippery stuff.

i   On the Elysée. On the University of Nanterre. In Piazza Navona. All over the road.

l   Is thrown out of the window by CIA agents. Is raped by paratroopers. Is killed by Australian aborigines.

m   With a gaping wound in the belly. Spewing forth streams of yellow (red, blue, black) paint. Making love with Voltaire.

n   Loquat.

o   Unsteadily. Very, very slowly. Remaining still while the background (process shot) moves.

p   Nanterre. Flins. Place de la Bastille. Clignancourt. Venice.

q   Jacques Servan-Schreiber. Jean-Paul Sartre. Pier Paolo Pasolini. D'Alembert.

r   Misses the train. Goes on a bicycle. On roller skates.

s   Bursts into tears. Shouts *Viva Guevara*.

t   A band of Indians.

u   Kill everybody. Kill nobody.

v   Quotations from Brecht. The Declaration of the Rights of Man. Saint-John Perse. Prince Korzybski. Eluard. Lo Sun. Charles Péguy. Rosa Luxemburg.

z   Diderot. Sade. Restif de la Bretonne. Pompidou.

w   A tomato. Red paint (blue, yellow, black).

x   Daniel Cohn-Bendit. Nixon. Madame de Sevigné. Voiture. Van Vogt. Einstein.

k   Goes away. Kills all the others. Throws a bomb at the Arc de Triomphe. Blows up an electronic brain. Empties onto the ground various cans of yellow (green, blue, red, black) paint.

j   The sayings of Mao. Writes a ta-tze-bao. Reads verses of Pierre Emmanuel. Watches a Chaplin movie.

y   The paratroopers. The Germans. Hordes of starving accountants brandishing sabers. Armored cars. Pier Paolo Pasolini with Pompidou. The Bank Holiday traffic. Diderot selling the Encyclopédie door to door. The Marxist-Leninist Union on skateboards.

Ermanno Olmi Scenario

A forester[a] out of work[b] roams at length[c] then comes back to his native village[d] and finds his mother[e] is dead.[f] He walks in the woods,[g] talks with a tramp[h] who understands[i] the beauty of the trees[l] and he remains there,[m] thinking.[n]

Variants Key

a   A young man who has just arrived in the city. A former partisan. A jaded executive. An Alpine soldier. A miner. A ski instructor.

b   Overworked. Sad. Without any purpose in life. Sick. Just fired. Overwhelmed by a feeling of emptiness. Who has lost his faith. Who has returned to the faith. After a vision of Pope John XXIII.

c   Briefly. Drives a mini Cooper along the superhighway. Is driving a truck from Bergamo to Brindisi.

d   To his brother's sawmill. To the mountain hut. To Pizzo Gloria. To Chamonix. To Lago di

Carezza. To Piazzale Corvetto and his cousin's tobacco shop.

e   Another close relative. Fiancée. Male friend. Parish priest.

f   Sick. Has become a prostitute. Has lost her faith. Has returned to the faith. Has had a vision of Pope John XXIII. Has left for France. Is lost in an avalanche. Is still performing the humble little daily tasks as always.

g   On the superhighway. Near the Idroscalo. At Rogoredo. Through immaculate snow. At San Giovanni sotto il Monte, Pope John XXIII's birthplace. In the halls of a totally alienated advertising agency.

h   With a former Alpine soldier. With the parish priest. With Monsignor Loris Capovilla. With a former partisan. With a mountain guide. With a ski instructor. With the head forester. With the executive of an industrial design studio. With a worker. With an unemployed southerner.

i   Doesn't understand. Remembers. Rediscovers. Learns thanks to a vision of Pope John XXIII.

l   Of the snow. Of the work site. Of solitude. Of friendship. Of silence.

m   Goes away forever.

n   Thinking of nothing. With no purpose in life now. With a new purpose in life. Making a novena to Pope John XXIII. Becoming a forester (mountain guide, tramp, miner, water bearer).

Angry Young Directors' Scenario

A young polio victim[x] of very rich[y] parents sits in a wheelchair[z] in a villa[n] with a park full of gravel.[k] He hates his cousin,[s] an architect[w] and a radical,[q] and has sexual congress[e] with his own mother[b] in the missionary position,[v] then kills himself[f] after first playing chess[a] with the farm manager.[j]

Variants Key

x   Paraplegic. Compulsive hysteric. Simple neurotic. Revolted by the neocapitalistic society. Unable to forget an act of sexual abuse at the age of three by his grandfather. With a facial tic. Handsome but impotent. Blond and lame (and unhappy about it). Pretending to be crazy. Pretending to be sane. With a religious mania. Enrolled in the Marxist-Leninist Union but for neurotic reasons.

y   Fairly well off. In decline. Diseased. Destroyed. Separated.

z   On cul-de-jatte. On crutches. With a wooden leg. With false teeth. With long fangs on which he leans. Supports himself by leaning against trees.

n   Yacht. Garden city. Sanatorium. Father's private clinic.

k   Another kind of paving, provided it makes a constant sound when a heavy vehicle arrives.

s   Other close relation, as desired, half brothers and in-laws admissible. Mother's lover (or father's, aunt's, grandmother's, farmer's, fiancée's).

w City planner. Writer. President of Save Venice. Stockbroker (successful). Left-wing political writer.

q Subscriber to the *New York Review*. Moderate Communist. Liberal professor. Former partisan leader. Member of WWF board. Friend of Theodorakis, Garry Wills, Jessica Mitford. Cousin of Berlinguer. Former leader of Student Movement.

e Tries to have sexual congress. Reveals impotence. Thinks of having sexual congress (dream sequence). Deflowers with bicycle pump.

b Grandmother, aunt, father, sister, female second cousin, female first cousin, sister-in-law, brother.

v From behind. Inserting a stick of dynamite into the vagina. With an ear of corn (must be preceded by casual Faulkner quotation from radical architect, see s-w). Cunnilingus. Beating her savagely. Wearing female dress. Dressing up to look like father (grandmother, aunt, mother, brother, cousin). Dressed as Fascist official. In U.S. Marine uniform. With plastic mask of Dracula. In SS uniform. In radical dress. In Scorpio Rising costume. In a Paco Rabanne tailleur. In prelate's robes.

f Sprinkles himself with gasoline. Swallows sleeping pills. Doesn't kill himself but thinks of killing himself (dream sequence). Kills her (him). Masturbates while singing "Love divine, all loves excelling." Calls the suicide hot line. Blows up the post office. Urinates on the family tomb.

Sets fire to photo of himself as a baby, with
savage laughter. Sings "Mira Norma."

a   Chinese checkers. Toy soldiers. Hide-and-seek.
Tag. Gin rummy. Slapjack. Racing demons. Fan-
tan. Snap. Spin the bottle.

j   His aunt. Grandmother. Innocent little sister.
Himself in the mirror. Dead mother (dream
sequence). The postman on his rounds. The old
housekeeper. Carmen Moravia. A Bellocchio
brother (according to preference).

Luchino Visconti Scenario

The Baroness,[a] a Hanseatic[b] lesbian, betrays her
male lover,[c] a worker at Fiat,[d] reporting him[e] to the
police.[f] He dies[g] and she repents[h] and gives a big
party,[i] orgiastic,[l] in the cellars of La Scala[m] with
transvestites,[n] and there poisons herself.[o]

Variants Key

a   Duchess. Daughter of the Pharaoh. Marquise.
Dupont stockholder. Middle European (male)
composer.

b   From Munich. Sicilian. Papal aristocracy. From
Pittsburgh.

c   Her female lover. Husband. Son with whom she
has an incestuous relationship. Sister with whom
she has an incestuous relationship. Lover of her
daughter with whom she has an incestuous relationship, though she betrays her daughter with
her daughter's male lover. The Oberkomman

danturweltanschaunggotterdammerungführer of the SA of Upper Silesia. The catamite of her impotent and racist husband.

d   A fisherman from the Tremiti Islands. Steelworker. Riverboat gambler. Mad doctor in a Nazi concentration camp. Commander of the Pharaoh's light cavalry. Aide-de-camp of Marshal Radetzsky. Garibaldi's lieutenant. Gondolier.

e   Giving him wrong directions about the route. Entrusting to him a bogus secret message. Summoning him to a cemetery on the night of Good Friday. Disguising him as Rigoletto's daughter and putting him in a sack. Opening a trapdoor in the great hall of the ancestral castle while he is singing Manon dressed up as Marlene Dietrich.

f   To Marshal Radetzsky. To the Pharaoh. To Tigellinus. To the Duke of Parma. To the Prince of Salina. To the Oberdeutscheskriminalinterpolphallusführer of the SS of Pomerania.

g   Sings an aria from *Aida*. Sets off in a fishing smack to reach Malta and is never heard from again. Is beaten with iron bars during a wildcat strike. Is sodomized by a squadron of uhlans under the command of the Prince of Homburg. Becomes infected during sexual contact with Vanina Vanini. Is sold as a slave to the Sultan and found again by the Borgia at the flea market of Portobello Road. Is used as a throw rug by the Pharaoh's daughter.

h   Is not the least repentant. Is wild with joy. Gone mad. Bathing at the Lido to the sound of balalaikas.

i   A big funeral. A satanic rite. A Te Deum of thanksgiving.

l   Mystical. Dramatic. Baroque. Algolagnical. Scatological. Sadomasochistic.

m   Père-Lachaise. Hitler's Bunker. In a castle in the Black Forest. In section 215 of the Fiat Mirafiori factory. At the Hôtel des Bains on the Lido at Venice.

n   With corrupt little boys. With German homosexuals. With the *Trovatore* chorus. With lesbians dressed as Napoleonic soldiers. With Cardinal Tisserant and Garibaldi. With Claudio Abbado. With Gustav Mahler.

o   Attends the entire Ring cycle. Plays ancient songs of Burgundy on a Jew's harp. Undresses at the climax of the party, revealing that she is really a man, then castrates herself. Dies of consumption, wrapped in Gobelin tapestries. Swallows liquid wax and is buried in the Musée Grévin. Has her throat cut by a lathe operator as she utters obscure prophecies. Waits for the *acqua alta* in St. Mark's square and drowns herself.

1972

The Phenomenology of
Mike Bongiorno

Translator's note: Mike Bongiorno, since the dawn of
Italian television, has been a star, mainly as the quizmaster
of programs based on—indeed, copied from—such American shows as "The $64,000 Question" and "Wheel of
Fortune." But to call him a star gives an inadequate idea.
Imagine someone with the popularity (but without the
vitality) of Johnny Carson and the anonymity of Ed Sul-
livan, with a touch of Sesame Street's Mr. Smiley. Even
English-speaking readers who have never seen Italian TV
will understand the type from Eco's analysis.

The man seduced by the mass media becomes, of his
peers, the most respected. He is never asked to be
anything beyond what he already is. He is never
encouraged to desire anything that does not conform
to his own tastes. Still, among the narcotic rewards
granted him is escape into daydreams, so he is often
confronted by goals which could create tension between them and him. He is, however, absolved of
every responsibility, because these goals are deliber-

ately placed outside his reach. The tension is resolved in identification and not in actual transformations aimed at altering the status quo. In short, he is asked to be a man with a refrigerator and a twenty-one-inch TV set: he is asked to remain as he is, in other words, merely adding, to the objects that he possesses, a refrigerator and a TV. In return he is offered role models like Kirk Douglas or Superman. The model of the mass-media consumer, on the other hand, is a superman that the consumer will never aspire to, though he enjoys identifying with that ideal in his imagination, as a person might put on someone else's clothes for a moment before a mirror, without the slightest notion of ever owning those clothes.

But television puts the consumer in a new position. Television does not propose *superman* as an ideal with which to identify: it proposes *everyman*. Television's ideal is the absolutely average person. In the theater Juliette Greco appears on the stage and immediately creates a myth and founds a cult; Josephine Baker prompts idolatrous rituals and gives her name to an era. In TV the magic face of Juliette Greco appears on various occasions, but the myth is never born; she is not the idol. The idol is the woman who announces her, and among women announcers the most beloved and famous will be the one who best embodies average characteristics: decent good looks, limited sex appeal, so-so taste, a certain house-wifely inexpressiveness.

Now, in the realm of quantitative phenomena, the average represents in fact a median, and for those who have not achieved it, it also represents a goal.

According to the famous *mot,* statistics is the science according to which if one man eats two chickens daily and another man eats none, then each has eaten one chicken. In reality, for the man who hasn't eaten the goal of one chicken a day, it is something to which he can aspire. But in the realm of qualitative phenomena, reducing to the median means reducing to zero. A man who possesses *all* the moral and intellectual virtues *to an average degree* immediately finds himself at a minimal level of development. The Aristotelian "mean" signifies equilibrium in the exercise of one's own passions, the passions balanced by the discriminating virtue of prudence. But one who harbors passions to an average degree and possesses an average prudence is a poor sample of humanity.

The most striking illustration of superman's being reduced to everyman is, in Italy, the figure of Mike Bongiorno and the history of his fame. Idolized by millions of people, this man owes his success to the fact that from every act, from every word of the persona that he presents to the telecameras there emanates an absolute mediocrity along with (the only virtue he possesses to a high degree) an immediate and spontaneous allure, which is explicable by the fact that he betrays no sign of theatrical artifice or pretense. He seems to be selling himself as precisely what he is, and what he is cannot create in a spectator, even the most ignorant, any sense of inferiority. Indeed, the spectator sees his own limitations glorified and supported by national authority.

To understand the extraordinary power of Mike Bongiorno it is necessary to conduct an analysis of his behavior, an authentic "Phenomenology of Mike Bongiorno," in which, of course, his name stands not for the real man but for the public figure.

Mike Bongiorno is not particularly good-looking, not athletic, courageous, or intelligent. Biologically speaking, he represents a modest level of adaptation to the environment. The hysterical love he arouses in teenage girls must be attributed partly to the maternal feelings he arouses in a female adolescent, and partly to the glimpse he allows her of an ideal lover, meek and vulnerable, gentle and considerate.

Mike Bongiorno is not ashamed of being ignorant and feels no need to educate himself. He comes into contact with the most dazzling areas of knowledge and remains virgin, intact, a consolation to others in their natural tendencies to apathy and mental sloth. He takes great care not to awe the spectator, demonstrating not only his lack of knowledge but also his firm determination to learn nothing.

On the other hand, Mike Bongiorno displays a sincere and primitive admiration for those who do know things. He emphasizes, however, their physical qualities, their dogged application, their power of memory, their obvious, elementary methodology. A man becomes cultivated by reading many books and retaining what they say. Mike Bongiorno hasn't the slightest inkling that culture has a critical and creative function. For him, its only criterion is quantitative. In this sense (having to read many books in order to

⌐ᵤ ᵤultured), the man with no natural gifts in that direction simply renounces the attempt.

Mike Bongiorno professes a boundless faith in the expert. A professor is a man of learning, a representative of official culture; he is the technician in the field. The question goes to him, to his authority.

But true admiration of culture is found only when, through culture, money is earned. Then culture proves to be of some use. The mediocre man refuses to learn, but he decides to make his son study.

Mike Bongiorno's notion of money and its value is petit bourgeois: "You've now won a hundred thousand lire! A tidy sum, eh?"

Mike Bongiorno thus expresses to the contestant the merciless reflections that the viewers will be making at home: "You must be very happy with all this money, considering the monthly salary you earn. Have you ever put your hands on so much money before?"

Like children, Mike Bongiorno thinks of people in categories and addresses them with comic deference (the child says, "Excuse me, Mr. Policeman . . ."), always using, however, the most common and vulgar category: "Mr. Garbage Collector," "Mr. Sharecropper."

Mike Bongiorno accepts all the myths of the society in which he lives. When Signora Balbiano d'Aramengo appears as a contestant, he kisses her hand, saying that he is doing this because she is a countess (sic).

With society's myths he accepts also society's conventions. He is paternal and condescending with the humble, deferential with the socially distinguished.

Handing out money, he instinctively thinks, without explicitly saying so, more in terms of alms than of deserved rewards. He indicates his belief that in the dialectic of the classes the one route of upward mobility is represented by Providence (which, on occasion, can assume the guise of Television).

Mike Bongiorno speaks a *basic* Italian. His speech achieves the maximum of simplicity. He abolishes the subjunctive, and subordinate clauses; he manages to make syntax almost invisible. He shuns pronouns, repeating always the whole subject. He employs an unusually large number of full stops. He never ventures into parentheses, does not use elliptical expressions or allusions. His only metaphors are those that now belong to the commonplace lexicon. His language is strictly referential and would delight a neo-positivist. No effort is required in order to understand him. Any viewer senses that he himself, if called upon, could be more talkative than Mike Bongiorno.

Mike Bongiorno rejects the idea that a question can have more than one answer. He regards all variants with suspicion. Nabucco and Nabuccodonosor are not the same thing. Confronted by data, he reacts like a computer, firmly convinced that A equals A and *tertium non datur*. An inadvertent Aristotelian, he is consequently a conservative pedagogue, paternalistic, reactionary.

Mike Bongiorno has no sense of humor. He laughs because he is happy with reality, not because he is capable of distorting reality. The nature of paradox-eludes him; if someone uses a paradox in speaking to him, he repeats it with an amused look and shakes his head, implying that his interlocutor is pleasantly eccentric. He refuses to suspect that behind the paradox a truth is concealed, and in any case he does not consider paradox an authorized vehicle of expression.

He avoids polemics, even in admissible fields. He does not lack for information on the oddities of the knowable (a new school of painting, an abstruse discipline . . . "Tell me now, I hear all this talk about Cubism. Just what is Cubism exactly?"). Having received the explanation, he does not try to delve any deeper, but indicates, on the contrary, his polite dissent, as a sensible, right-thinking citizen. Still, he respects the opinion of others, not for any ideological reason but out of lack of interest.

From all the possible questions on a subject, he chooses the one that would first come to anybody's mind and that half the viewers would immediately reject as too banal: "What is this picture about?" "What made you pick a hobby so different from your regular job?" "What got you interested in philosophy?"

He drives clichés to their extreme. A girl educated by nuns is virtuous; a girl with brightly colored stockings and a ponytail is a "hippy." He asks the former if she, a nice girl, would like to look like the latter; when he is told that the question is insulting, he consoles the second girl, praising her physical superiority and humiliating the convent-school product. In this dizzying whirl of *faux pas* he doesn't even try to paraphrase, for paraphrase is already a form of wit, and wit belongs to a Vico cycle alien to Bongiorno. For him, everything has one name and only one; any rhetorical figure is a fraud. In the final analysis, a *faux pas* stems always from an act of unintentional sincerity; when the sincerity is deliberate, what results is not a *faux pas* but a challenge, a provocation. The *faux pas* (of which Bongiorno is a past master, according to critics and audience) arises precisely when the speaker is sincere by mistake, out of thoughtlessness. The more mediocre a man is, the clumsier he is. Mike Bongiorno is a consolation to the mediocre, for he exalts the *faux pas*, raising it to the dignity of rhetoric, of an etiquette established by the TV company and by the viewing nation.

Mike Bongiorno sincerely rejoices with the victor, because he honors success. Politely uninterested in the loser, he is moved if the latter is in desperate straits, and he may promote some beneficent action, at the conclusion of which he expresses his satisfaction and convinces the audience of his pleasure; then he moves on to other concerns, content with the fact that this is the best of all possible worlds. He is unaware of the tragic dimension of life.

Mike Bongiorno therefore convinces the public, by his living and triumphant example, of the value of mediocrity. He provokes no inferiority complexes, though he presents himself as an idol; and the public repays him, gratefully, with its love. He is an ideal that nobody has to strive for, because everyone is already at its level. No religion has ever been so indulgent to its faithful. In him the tension between what is and what should be is annulled. He says to his worshipers, "You are God, stay exactly as you are."

1961

My Exagmination

*Round His Factification for Incamination
to Reduplication with Ridecolation of a
Portrait of the Artist as Alessandro Manzoni*

The reviewer cannot conceal his satisfaction in speaking about this little volume from the pen of Mr. James Joyce, now printed for the first time by Shakespeare & Co., revived by Miss Beach solely to permit this literary event, which I suspect will be hailed as by far the most important of the year. While we must be grateful to Miss Beach for giving us back, not without sacrifice on her part, her estimable publishing house of the twenties, we owe an even deeper gratitude to Richard Ellmann and his collaborators, who after years of unceasing study of manuscripts preserved at the University of Buffalo have succeeded in collating this work (which Mr. Joyce wrote during the period in which he taught Triestine dialect at the Berlitz School in Como), though the author himself never chose to establish a definitive redaction. It is easy to understand how this situation led scholars to make the deplorable error of considering the manuscript lost or, as I suspect was the case with many, that its existence was questionable, a thing beyond verification.

As I hold this work in my hands today, I cannot help but doubt the rationality of such suspicions (though the scholars' philological caution is certainly praiseworthy). At the same time I hope to be allowed to venture a critical approach to this work, which follows *Finnegans Wake*—and follows it not only in the chronological sense. The sensible reader may realize, in studying this volume, that it represents a rather advanced point in Joycean development: only after having attempted the colossal experiment with language in his preceding work could Mr. Joyce succeed, once he had "rinsed his garments in the waters of the Liffey," in writing this book, *I promessi sposi (The Betrothed)*.

The title of this work is eloquent, and the reviewer needs add little comment to it, as it is rich in profoundly revelatory allusions.

If *Finnegans Wake* was the "work in progress" of which all Joyceans were given news in the course of its evolution, *I promessi sposi* is the "promised work," like the Promised Land desired by the Jewish people (the people of Leopold Bloom, we must remember). But *this* promise is fulfilled, inasmuch as a marriage takes place, the union of the youthful aspirations of Stephen Dedalus and the *radiance* and the scholastic *proportio*. the union of the dazzling linguistic gifts of the *vicocyclometer* of maturity and lyric style and drama and epic, of the language of tradition and the languages of the future, as linguistic experimentation is wedded to the narrative construction of the works of youth.

Thus we feel that in the light of this final work the nature and function of its predecessor are clarified, and the *Wake,* the mourning vigil of Tim Finnegan, is seen for what it really is: the nuptial vigil of Renzo and Lucia.

I promessi sposi begins where *Finnegan* ends, and it begins by picking up the theme of the liquid element on which *Finnegan* concludes: Riverrun. The novel begins with the description of a body of water and with a parodistic subtlety of which only an Irishman could be capable; it begins by exactly imitating the earlier work. How, in fact, does *I promessi sposi* begin? Allow me to quote: "That branch of the lake of Como, which extends southwards, between two uninterrupted chains of mountains, and is all inlets and bays, as those same mountains project or recede, suddenly narrows, assuming the flow and form of a river, between a promontory on one side and a broad shore opposite . . ."

The opening of *Finnegan* was similar. Its first sentence, if we eliminate all the linguistic ambiguities that encumber it, goes like this: "That course of the river that, having passed the church of Adam and Eve, from the turn of the beach to the curve of the bay, leads us along a more comfortable route of return again to Howth Castle and environs . . ."

But in *I promessi sposi* the language has been further refined; the allusions are more subtle, less visible, the symbolism more powerful and pure.

Abandoning the midnight in which the dream of H. C. Earwicker concluded (and in which the nocturnal monologue of Molly Bloom concluded also), the lake of Como turns toward the noon of the south, but in the form of a "branch," this immediately recalling, thanks to the anthropological intervention of Frazer, the "bough" and the rites of fertility and rebirth.

In her rebirth in a new day's light, Anna Liffey has become a lake (expanding into the image of the maternal womb), and Anna Livia, now a mature woman, image of Demeter, all bosom and belly, can then contract again and resume her course and form as a river, beginning another story. "Resume her course," because with the new story a new course begins, among the many fluxes and refluxes that are woven into the human story of which *Finnegan* is meant to be a condensation.

The work's narrative scheme is disturbingly simple; in a sense, it acts as the antistrophe of the plot of *Ulysses*. In that book, the apparent description of a single day in the life of Leopold Bloom was transformed as it proceeded into a discussion of a whole city and of the universe. Here the apparently complex tale of a series of historical events involving an entire region and an empire (the Spanish) concerns in reality the events of a single day in the life of the protagonist, Renzo Tramaglino.

One morning at dawn, as he is preparing to celebrate his marriage to his promised bride, Lucia Mondella, Renzo learns from the village pastor, Don Abbondio, that the local feudal lord, Don Rodrigo, is opposed to the marriage. After a quarrel with the pastor, Renzo and Lucia flee from the village with the aid of a Capuchin monk, Fra Cristoforo. While Lucia seeks refuge in a convent in Monza, Renzo goes to Milan. There, that afternoon, the youth is involved in an uprising and therefore must escape to Bergamo, as Lucia, through the complicity of a nun, Gertrude, is abducted by another feudal lord known as the Unnamed. The Cardinal of Milan intervenes, however, to liberate her. At sunset a plague breaks out in Milan, which kills Don Rodrigo, Don Abbondio, and Padre Cristoforo. Renzo that evening hastily returns from Bergamo and finds Lucia safe and sound, wherefore he and she can be joined in marriage during the night. This is the story, condensed, as we have seen, into the twenty-four hours of one day; but Joyce conceals the initial scheme (secretly confided by him to Stuart Gilbert), confusing and mixing the events in such a way that the reader has the impression of an unnatural and complex temporal development.

Yet the development is actually quite simple and linear, and to perceive it in all its purity it must be subjected to a reading shorn of pseudointellectual complications, where one merely underscores, in each episode, the basic symbol, the corresponding profession, and the reference to the animal world.

PART ONE. From dawn to early afternoon, 6 A.M. to 2 P.M. Renzo Tramaglino is about to marry Lucia Mondella, when Don Abbondio informs him that Don Rodrigo desires Lucia and is opposed to the wedding. Renzo asks advice of a pettifogging lawyer, but realizing that all attempts are in vain, he and Lucia flee with the help of Padre Cristoforo. Lucia takes refuge in a convent in Monza, Renzo goes to Milan. *Symbol of this Part:* the pastor. *Profession:* weaving. *Animal:* the capon, emblem of impotence and castration.

PART TWO. Afternoon, 2 to 5 P.M. Renzo in Milan becomes involved in an uprising and must escape to Bergamo. Lucia is abducted by the Unnamed, through the complicity of Gertrude. The Cardinal of Milan liberates Lucia and places her in the custody of a scholar, Don Ferrante, and his wife, Donna Prassede. *Symbol:* the nun. *Profession:* library science. *Animal:* the mule, emblem of obstinacy (of the villains).

PART THREE. Sunset and evening, 5 P.M. to midnight. The plague breaks out in Milan, and Don Rodrigo, Don Abbondio, and Padre Cristoforo die. Renzo returns to Milan from Bergamo and finds Lucia safe and sound. Finally reunited, they marry. *Symbol:* the gravedigger. *Profession:* hospital management. *Animal:* does not exist, because evil is defeated. In the place of the animal there is purifying rain, which recalls the initial theme of water, as well as the washerwomen in *Finnegan* (Anna Livia Plurabelle episode).

I would be misleading the reader if I said that the author presents this linear scheme in all its aspects and makes it easily recognizable in the body of the story. Actually, this simple tale in itself is insignificant, and in the course of the novel it is masked and hidden, so the reader has the impression that the events cover a much greater period of time; but I cannot express adequately my admiration for this clever fictional structure, which creates substantial indecision and ambiguity in space-time, convincing us that the events take place in the Lombard plain, whereas, in fact, if I am not trivially distorting the author's intentions, everything happens in Dublin.

In the continuous and amiable dialogue—and every now and then it becomes poetry, from Donne to the Elizabethans to Spenser—that unfolds between tradition and the individual talent, the first rule for a selective and fertile imagination, I believe, is to produce a good work. To write something valid and enduring is still the best homage that can be rendered to poetry, and if I use the word "profitable," it is because I can find no better term to express the advantage humanity derives from the existence of a good work of poetry. We achieve poetry when the imagination knows it has arrived at that condition of significant emotion whereby it is capable of creation. In my previous essays I may have professed a somewhat different and more superficial view of the problem, but I have reviewed it with great attention and feel I cannot say anything less specific. This brief digression has perhaps caused us to stray from the subject of Mr. Joyce's book; but I believe it was necessary in order to clarify a point that has left the critic legitimately puzzled on more than one occasion (the ideal critic is a figure I could not define with absolute confidence, but I am convinced a critic cannot be ideal if he lacks the capacity of conducting a convincing critical discourse on a given poetic text). Now, to return to Mr. Joyce's book, I further believe that simplicity and autonomy of image is still the best way for a text to speak to the reader, without his being led to superimpose complicated and toilsome keys to the reading—vitiated, in the final analysis, by an intellectualism that is death to poetry.

Making a concerted effort to grasp the so-called plot, asking oneself, while reading a story, what is happening and how it will end—asking oneself, *enfin*, as the academic does when reading a mystery, who did it—takes three quarters of the pleasure from the reading of a novel, and robs the art of four quarters of its *raison d'être*. So we would consider our purpose as critic achieved if we succeeded in convincing the reader to return to the fresh spontaneity with which the primitive reader—and with this term I mean the "natural reader" that modern industrial civilization is fast destroying—catches immediately, in the reading, all the allusions to the latest findings of structural anthropology or to Jungian archetypes without trying to superimpose over-intellectual explanations, and understands without travail the links between a character and the mystic figure of the Indian *schelm* according to Kerenyi. With the simplicity of leafing through an old family album at home, such a reader enjoys every correspondence—so immediately perceptible—between the syntactic structure and the structure of the universe according to the *Zohar*. He is not confounded, in the thrall of false scientific conceit, by a wish to see in the novel, at all costs, the story of a marriage opposed, but, rather, accepts in all its perspicuity the free engagement of Freudian submeanings playfully stratified in the connective tissue of the work, with no cultivated, Byzantine concern.

For this reason we would warn the reader against any ambiguously philosophizing interpretation that uses several hundred pages to explain the novel as, in fact, the story of a young man and a young woman anxious to celebrate their wedding but suffering obstacles placed in their path by a villain. It is impossible not to see in this hermeneutical superfetation an attempt to reduce all the dialectic of the work to a sexual foundation, identifying the relationship between the two characters as (vulgar and tediously trite!) erotic polarity, and therefore complicating outrageously the comprehension of the novel. Whereas with great clarity and the simplicity that only the great artist possesses, even the least prepared reader can readily observe a whole series of symbols pointing to the textile industry and matrilocal residence, and the constant presence of Agnese as a *basso ostinato* expressing the reality of the *Mutterrecht* (even the most innocent reader will note the explicit influence of Bachofen in the figure of this "mother" who bears such weight in the book's conclusion, carrying around the children of Renzo and Lucia and "implanting kisses on their cheeks, which left a white mark for some time"!). The "diriment impediments" to which Don Abbondio symbolically alludes to dissuade Renzo from marrying are obviously a mere transfiguration of the *customs of avoidance* expounded by Tylor. Here the poet rediscovers them as archetypal probability, recurrent and profound, betrayed by the superficially canonical expressions with which the pastor conceals his intention to prevent a relationship between kin (kin in that they are "promised"), and you therefore cannot fail to understand the words *"Error, conditio, votum, cognatio, crimen, cultus disparitas, vis, ordo, ligamen, honestas, si sis affinis . . ."*

Similarly, despite the rivers of ink that have been spilled to place in a complicated and preternatural light Padre Cristoforo's farewell to the now reunited betrothed (end of Chapter XXVI)—"Oh, dear father, will we meet again?" "Up above, I hope"— how easy it is for the simple and spontaneous reader to catch the obvious reference to the *Corpus Hermeticum* and its basic dictate, *sicut inferius sic superius,* as anyone who in his childhood has so much as glanced at the works of Trismegistus will know.

Now, it is precisely the "gestural" immediacy of these images, their deployment according to a shrewd communicative strategy, the spontaneous emotive *pattern*, that stimulates and provides the reader with the enjoyment proper to reading. Thus he can follow, for example, the demure yet bold play of plot in which an opposition unfolds between the two poles of sexual congress and impotence as existential situation. It will be seen how through the character of Renzo the theme of castration as non-congress is handled, beginning with the capons he takes to the lawyer, a symbol too obvious to require commentary, then continuing with the young man's escape across the lake (escaping, he evades sexual commitment, and he does this through the archetype of exile, a clear reference to Thomas Mann's Joseph) and his flight to Bergamo, in which a great quantity of revealing symbols is condensed. Renzo's castration is opposed by the phallic figure of the mountain, which dominates Lucia's stream of consciousness, her interior monologue as she crosses the lake at night. Here we find a free association of images counterpointed by the presence of water, which assumes the form of a furrow continually closing upon itself then opened again by human intervention: "The measured slap of those two oars that sliced the blue surface of the lake, abruptly emerged dripping, and plunged in again." Here is an image that while patently sexual at the same time suggests in explicitly Bergsonian terms an *élan vital* that, striking at the marrow of being and then passing on, is realized as psychic *durée*, as furrow: "The wave marked by the boat, meeting again behind the poop, traced a wrinkled stripe, which was moving away from the shore." Now Lucia's monologue, made possible by the presence of the water as duration, as psychic texture, a storehouse of elements (Thales) of a being reduced to memory, focuses almost exclusively on the image of the mountains, whose loss she regrets and which, in a process typical of the unconscious with an arguable manifestation of an Oedipus complex, are identified with the paternal image ("unequal peaks, known to those who have grown up in your midst, and impressed in her mind, no less than the aspect of her closest family . . ."). Deprived of the union symbolized by the mountain as phallic reality, Lucia—in a succession of images that at times achieves the impressive power of Molly Bloom's nocturnal monologue, of which this is admittedly a minor but not unworthy copy—feels "disgusted and weary": "The air seems to her burdensome and dead as she advances sad and absent in the tumultuous cities; the houses after houses, the streets opening into other streets seem to take her breath away." Anyone can see the evident expressionistic derivation of these last images (Kafka is one of the first names that come to mind) as well as the distinct influence of the most recent descriptive techniques of the *nouveau roman* (the description of those houses after houses and streets that become other streets all too clearly shows the mark of the Butor of *L'Emploi du temps* and the Robbe-Grillet of *Le Labyrinthe*).

What now happens to Renzo, fleeing to Bergamo? The *calembour* contained in the name of the city is self-evident: the word has two roots, one Germanic (*Berg*, mountain) and the other Greek (*gamos*, wedding). Bergamo represents, in fact, Renzo's final attempt to restore his lost sexuality, as he yearns for symbolic marriage with the very symbol of it—but in so doing, in desiring that same symbol of his potency, he redirects his travail in an ambiguous homosexual ambiance, a clear and harmonious antistrophe to the equally ambiguous rapport that at the same time Lucia is establishing with the nun of

Monza. Nor must we forget that Mr. Joyce, who lived for such a long time in Trieste, could not be ignorant of the sexual significance of the root *mona,* which we encounter once more, note, both in *monaca* (nun), with whom Lucia deals, and in *monatti* (the removers of corpses from the hospital, surrounding Lucia, when Renzo finds her there).

It is obvious, then, that with the greatest simplicity of means Mr. Joyce has managed here to penetrate into the deepest recesses of the human spirit, revealing its secret contradictions and realizing (triumph of ambiguity) in both leading characters the archetype of the androgyne. It is Lucia who in Chapter XXXVI accepts with joy the proposal of Padre Cristoforo, or, rather, his perceptive insinuation ("If it ever seemed to me that two people were united by God, you two were they: now I do not see why God would wish to separate you"), and, asking to be united with Renzo, she realizes in modern form the myth of Salmakis, which takes on further implications if we recall that in this same chapter Padre Cristoforo, uttering the above hermetic declaration, undoubtedly refers to the neoplatonic divinity, whereby the union of the two characters becomes the figure of a cosmic union, a kabbalistic *cingulum Veneris,* in which the very personality of the characters and their sexual individuality are joined in a higher unity. The unity is achieved, the author suggests, because in straightforward neoplatonic terms every impurity ceases; and in fact the decease of Padre Cristoforo (etymologically *christos fero,* and therefore "bearer of the anointed"), who comes to stand for impurity (there is in Padre Cristoforo the burden of an original sin, a youthful crime), coincides with the rainfall and therefore with water, the generating and enveloping principle, the unity of the higher Sephirot, Anna Livia Plurabelle. The cycle is closed.

This is the substance of the book, or at least what emerges from a first reading, for those who are reluctant to look for further hidden meanings beyond those that the narrative immediacy of the images offers. But there are infinite subtle correspondences still to be pointed out! Think of the presence of the Unnamed, who suggests with such force the figure of the stranger in the mackintosh in *Ulysses*! And the parallel between the episode of the library and Mr. Magee (again in *Ulysses*) and the library of Don Ferrante! Or between the argument of Bloom in the tavern and that of Renzo, both men victims of a "law-abiding citizen"! Or between Lucia's night in the castle of the Unnamed and Stephen Dedalus's night in the brothel of Bella Cohen (who corresponds also to the figure of the "old woman" who receives Lucia)!

Such observations might lead us to speak of *I promessi sposi* as a minor work, a clever rehash of themes and images already exploited in previous works, but the novel, clearly demanding these back-references, becomes instead the summation and conclusion of all the preceding oeuvre. Must we then say that it represents the apex of the Joycean canon? Perhaps not, but it does represent its fulfilment.

As we live in an odd country, where common sense occasionally assumes the eccentric forms of madness, there will surely be those who try to read this book in a thousand different keys, one more absurd than the next. Father Noon, S. J., will no doubt offer his interpretation, as he has interpreted Mr. Joyce's previous work, seeking again to put this volume in a religious context, perhaps essaying (if we may prophesy) a definition of *I promessi sposi* as a novel of Providence.

Worse still, there will be no dearth of pseudo-intellectual interpretations that attempt to see these archetypal symbols as so many "narrative characters," even referring to a so-called Joycean realism. And we strongly suspect that there will be those who dwell on the beauty of the language without bearing in mind that every expression, every image here is "beautiful" because it connotes a richer symbolic reality. But the temptation to aesthetic distortion is always present in criticism as in contemporary poetry, and thus it is difficult to know how to read a book. We therefore conclude this review of ours, which is also an invitation to direct and immediate contact with the text, by citing a statement made a few years ago by Ezra Pound when he commented on some verses of a little poem printed by the firm of Faber & Faber, *The Divine Comedy:* "Rarely is clarity a gift of the poet, and for one vorticist like Cavalcanti we will always find ten academics bloated with culture like Burchiello. This means that Usury nests always in our midst, but there is always the lucidity of a phanopoeia that can save us. Why then spend four complex words—*dolce colore d'oriental zaffiro*—where it would have been so much more immediate and comprehensible to use the corresponding Chinese ideogram?"

1962